Have Atheists Proved
There Is No God?

Thomas B. Warren, Ph.D.

Professor of Philosophy of Religion and Apologetics
Harding Graduate School of Religion
Memphis, Tennessee

NATIONAL CHRISTIAN PRESS, INC.
P. O. Box 1001
Jonesboro, Arkansas 72401

To

B. C. GOODPASTURE,

valiant soldier of the cross

Acknowledgments

I wish to acknowledge with gratitude the permission of the following publishers to reprint in this book material from the following copyright works controlled by them.

Harper and Row, New York: from John Hick, *Evil and the God of Love,* 1966.

Harper and Row, New York, Harper Torchbooks: from "God, Evil, and Immortality" in *Religion from Tolstoy to Camus,* ed. by Walter Kaufmann, 1961.

Harper and Brothers, New York: from Nels F. S. Ferré, *Evil and the Christian Faith,* 1947.

Abingdon-Cokesbury Press, New York: from Edwin Lewis, *Great Christian Teachings,* 1933.

The University Press, Cambridge: from Fredrick R. Tennant, *Philosophical Theology,* 2 volumes, 1956.

Eerdmans Publishing Company, Grand Rapids: from *The Writings of the Ante-Nicene Fathers,* Vol. I, Edinburgh, 1867. Ed. A. Roberts and J. Donaldson, 1885.

Doubleday and Company, Inc., Garden City, New York: from Austin Farrer, *Love Almighty and Ills Unlimited,* 1961.

Prentice-Hall, Inc., Englewood Cliffs, New Jersey: from John Hick, *Philosophy of Religion,* 1963.

Hafner Publishing Company, Inc., Darien, Conn.: from David Hume's "Dialogues Concerning Natural Religion" *God and Evil,* ed. by Nelson Pike, 1964. (Permission granted from J. L. Mackie.)

Prentice-Hall, Inc., Englewood Cliffs, New Jersey: from J. L. Mackie "Evil and Omnipotence," *God and Evil,* ed. by Nelson Pike, 1964. (Permission granted from "Mind" magazine; Gilbert Ryle, editor, through J. L. Mackie.)

Moody Press, Moody Bible Institute of Chicago, Illinois: from Stuart Hackett, *The Resurrection of Theism,* 1957.

Introduction

In this series of lectures, I plan to talk about theism and atheism of very particular kinds. The word "theism" is used by some to refer to belief in something or someone other than the infinite God of Christian faith. But, when I use the term "theism" in this series, I will be referring to *Biblical* theism— that is, I will be referring to faith in and obedience to the God described in the *Bible*. I will *not* be referring to everything that is *called* theism. There are many viewpoints which are *called* theism which are *not* in harmony with the Biblical view of God.

There are theologians and philosophers who claim to be in the tradition of Judeo-Christian theism (as Biblical theism is sometimes called) but who hold views which conflict with the Bible view of God. As a preliminary consideration, in this series of lectures, the expression "theism" will be used with a very definite reference; that is, it will be used to refer to the traditional view that God is "the infinite, eternal, uncreated personal reality, who has created all that exists other than himself, and who has revealed himself to his human creatures as holy and living."[1] This view entails the claim that God is *personal;* that he thinks, loves, hates, makes decisions, can hear and respond to the prayers of his creature, man. With reference to the *world,* the view entails the further claim that God is both immanent in the world and yet transcends the world, that he cannot be identified with the world yet is concerned with the world. God is the ultimate *source* of all reality other than himself. Obviously, such a view of God is in

---

[1] As summarized in John Hick, *Philosophy of Religion* (Englewood Cliffs: Prentice-Hall, Inc., 1963), p. 14. (Hereinafter referred to as POR)

conflict with a number of views the exponents of which recognize themselves to be devotees of Judeo-Christian theism.

It may be the case that no one can set out an absolutely perfect, fully comprehensive definition of God. Perhaps one would be correct in holding that God is beyond man's complete and absolute comprehension. But no theist should be willing to be recklessly, or even deliberately, vague. Thus it seems that at the very least the theist should be willing to give a clear account of what he does *not* mean when he uses the term "God." Later in the series I shall be giving much more detail about the various attributes of God. However, at this point, in viewing these matters as being involved in a merely preliminary definition of God, I will set out some of the things which are *not* meant when I use the term "God" in this series of lectures.

In this series of lectures when I say "theism" I will be referring to a view which is in conflict with that of the theologians and philosophers who espouse a *naturalistic* theory of religion and who view God not as conscious (and thus personal) but as the dynamic, internal structuring principle in the universe. Naturalism, in effect, denies the existence of the God described in the pages of the Bible.

The term "God" as used in this series is also in conflict with so-called *finitism,* the view that God is definitely limited in some attribute such as: power, goodness, knowledge, etc. A deity which is limited by factors which arise outside of his own nature is quite clearly not the source of all reality other than itself (or himself), and is thus not "God" in the sense in which that term will be used by me in these lectures.

Neither is "God" to be identified with the world nor the world with God, as is done by *Pantheists.* Pantheism is in conflict with the view that God is the source of the world and thus transcends the world.

And it is clear that "theism" as I use it here, is in conflict with the view that there is only one existent, the absolute, with this one existent being the true subject of all significant propositions. "God," as used by me in these lectures, is the source of the world and is thus not all that exists.

When I use the word "God" I shall be referring to that eternal, self-existent being who is infinite in all of his attributes: infinite in power, infinite in love and goodness, infinite in knowledge and wisdom, infinite in presence, etc.

When I use "atheist" during this series, I shall be referring to those thinkers who not only are not convinced of the existence of the infinite God, but who hold that there is adequate evidence in the world to warrant the conclusion that God does *not* exist. Thus it is clear that atheism is not the same as agnosticism. Agnostics claim that there is not adequate evidence to warrant either conclusion (that is, that God *does* exist or that God does *not* exist), so they simply suspend judgment—as their appellative implies that they would. They claim that neither they nor anyone else can really know whether God exists.

THE BASIC TOOL OF THE ATHEIST

Since atheists claim to be able to prove that the infinite God of the Bible does not exist, the vital question is: From what evidence do they draw such a conclusion?

It is likely the case that no charge has been made with greater frequency or with more telling force against theism of the Judeo-Christian (Biblical) tradition than that such theism is unable to explain adequately the occurrence or the existence of evil. For some men the idea of omnipotent, omnibenevolent (perfectly good) God is simply ruled out by the enormous depth and far-reaching extent of human suffering and moral evil which these men at least *think* they see in the world. Having been thus affected by what they conceive to be "evil," such men are disposed toward either atheism (or, perhaps, toward agnosticism) and toward some naturalistic theory of religion.

To most men there at least *seems* to exist an enormous amount of *evil* on earth. Although some have denied the *real* existence of evil, to many men the existence of evil, both in human experience and in the world itself, seems too self-evident to be rationally denied. It is sometimes pointed out that even those who claim that evil is only an illusion are still faced with the necessity of answering the question as to whether or not the illusion itself is an evil. Some hold that there is validity to the claim that a single instance of a nail piercing the human foot or the occurrence of a single selfish thought would be enough to prove the existence of evil. And so, some contend, rather than there being no "evil" at all, it seems clear that there *is* evil and that man suffers from: inanimate nature, animate nature, and from sin (that of others as well as his own). At times pain and suffering from these sources come upon men in what at least seems to be enormous amounts. Another factor which is very perplexing to many people is the fact that such misery (as I have just described) seems to fall upon individuals in such a haphazard fashion—that is, it falls upon the innocent and the righteous as well as upon the wicked.

As to the miseries which have come upon men from inanimate nature, it must be noted that thousands have been maimed or killed and millions of dollars worth of property has been destroyed by the power of such phenomena as hurricanes, tornadoes, earthquakes, floods, droughts, heat waves, blizzards, and falling stones and trees.

In the second place much pain and suffering have been inflicted upon many human beings by animal life. Innocent children have been terribly maimed or destroyed by ferocious wild beasts. Men, women, and children have suffered from the bites of various insects and reptiles. Animals themselves have been maimed and/or destroyed by other animals.

Men also suffer at the hands of other individual men. By the telling of a malicious falsehood, one man may destroy the reputation (and, thus, the happiness and peace of mind) of another. Women (and even very young and innocent girls) have been raped and murdered by lustful and/or perverted

men. Men destroy other men by the use of
knives, clubs, and firearms. There is ⌐
ence on the part of some men to t⌐
fellowmen stand in need of even the ⌐
men can see others starve for lack of fo⌐
clothing and shelter and, having no co⌐
nothing when they themselves have an abu⌐
cessities.

Much misery is also brought upon mankii⌐
of nations. Nations wage indescribably destruc⌐
other nations. By such wars women are left wido⌐
dren are left orphans. In addition to the thousan⌐
some case millions) of soldiers who die in such wars,
vilians (including women and children) are horribly ⌐
or killed. Enormous amounts of property are destroye⌐

Men also suffer because of their own weaknesses and
ures. Men live in violation of the moral code which th⌐
themselves believe they *ought* to obey. They thus bring upo⌐
themselves much suffering and anguish.

Another perplexing factor in this whole affair is that of the
seemingly chaotic nature of the *distribution* of suffering. It is
not only the *guilty* who suffer; *innocent* children suffer at
times even worse than do those who are the most degenerate.
It is not only the guilty who die; even very young children suffer and die. It is not only the strong (those who seem able to
bear such) who suffer; weak little children sometimes suffer
with such intensity as to break the heart of the most hardened
adult. The question might well then be raised: why do the
innocent suffer?

As a sort of corollary to the preceding, another very perplexing factor in this problem is that some people view much
of the suffering in the world as meaningless. Such thinkers
hold that, even if on *some* grounds it might be granted that
God would be justified with allowing *some* evil, there is such
an *overplus* of suffering as to make the possibility of the exist-

an omnipotent, omnibenevolent God simply incredi-

ese, and other elements of the problem which seem to
nd men, all combine to produce such a mass of human
xity as to cause some men to conclude that the existence
ch evil warrants the conclusion that one can be *certain*
such a God does not exist. This claim is made because of
conviction (held by some) that the affirmation of three
opositions which are basic to Christian faith ("God is omnip-
ent" "God is omnibenevolent" and "evil exists.") involves
logical contradiction. A logical contradiction occurs when
it is logically impossible for both of two statements to be true.
Thus, to say that two propositions: "God exists" and "Evil exists" involve a logical contradiction is to say that it is logically
impossible for them *both* to be true. If this claim is true, then
the espousal of Biblical theism involves the affirmation of a
logical contradiction. Since the affirmation of a logical contradiction implies that any proposition whatever can be true, if
this claim is true it would be destructive to Biblical theism.
This is the case because the logical contradiction could be
viewed as implying the following proposition, "Biblical theism
is false and should thus be rejected by everyone," as well as
the following proposition, "Traditional Biblical theism is
true." So, if the affirmation of the three basic propositions
noted above does indeed involve a logical contradiction, then
no rational man can affirm all three of them and remain such
a theist. To be sure, there are some problems which do not
actually invalidate belief in God for the reason that they simply are beyond man's knowledge. But the challenge pre-
sented by some men in their use of the so-called "problem of
evil" is such as to *demand* that the rational man either find
some way of meeting that challenge or else reject (or renounce) such theism. It is difficult, if indeed not impossible,
to imagine a challenge with more significance and implications.

Contents

xi

Appreciation

This book is basically the last chapter of the doctoral dissertation which I wrote at Vanderbilt University. The title of that dissertation is *God and Evil: Does Judeo-Christian Theism Involve a Logical Contradiction?* I have changed the wording here and there and made a few additions but no viewpoint has been changed at all from the views set out in the dissertation.

Since this book is based upon that dissertation, I wish to express my gratitude for aid extended to me by Professors Charles E. Scott, John J. Compton and Clement J. Dore, all of the Department of Philosophy, Vanderbilt University. Professor Scott guided me through the entire matter of selecting the problem, doing the necessary research, and the writing of the thesis. Both Professor Compton and Professor Dore made suggestions which were crucial to the final form which the dissertation took. Of course, no position which I affirm in this book is to be assigned to them because of the counsel they gave me.

THOMAS B. WARREN

Chapter 1

A Brief Look At The Problem of Evil
As Viewed By Some Thinkers

J. L. Mackie, an Australian philosopher, holds that in spite of the fact that traditional arguments for the existence of God have all been criticized and, he implies, refuted,[2] theologians can accept the criticism without losing their faith. This they can do, Mackie holds, by simply admitting that no rational proof of the existence of God can be sustained. He holds that the theologian can admit this and *still* hold on to all that is essential to theistic faith by contending that the existence of God can be shown in some *other* way; that is, in some *non-rational* way.[3]

Referring to the criticisms of the traditional arguments for the existence of God, Mackie says,

> I think, however, that a more telling criticism can be made by way of the traditional problem of evil. Here it can be shown, not that religious beliefs lack rational support, but that they are positively irrational, that the several parts of the essential theological doctrine are inconsistent with one another, so that the theologian can maintain his position as a whole only by a much more extreme rejection of reason than in the former case. He must now be prepared to believe not merely what cannot be proved, but what can be *disproved* from other beliefs that he also holds.[4]

[2]A claim which I deny.
[3]J. L. Mackie, "Evil and Omnipotence," in Nelson Pike, ed., *God and Evil* (Englewood Cliffs: Prentice-Hall, 1964), p. 46.
[4]*Ibid.,* pp. 46, 47.

1

Mackie further explicates the problem when he explains for whom the problem arises,

> The problem of evil, in the sense in which I shall be using the phrase, is a problem only for someone who believes that there is a god who is both omnipotent and wholly good.[5]

Mackie then explains just what kind of problem it is and is not.

> And it is a logical problem, the problem of clarifying and reconciling a number of beliefs: it is not a scientific problem that might be solved by further observations, or a practical problem that might be solved by a decision or an action.[6]

Mackie tells why he raises these points.

> . . . I mention them only because they are sometimes ignored by theologians, who sometimes pary a statement of problems with such remarks as, 'Well, can you solve the problem yourself?' or 'This is a mystery which will be revealed to us later' or 'Evil is something to be faced, and overcome, not to be merely discussed.'[7]

He holds that the simplest way of stating the problem is:

> . . . God is omnipotent: God is wholly good; and yet evil exists. There seems to be some contradiction between these three propositions so that if any two of them were true the third would be false. But at the same time all three are essential parts of most theological positions; the theologian it seems, at once *must* adhere and *cannot* consistently adhere to all three.[8]

Mackie admits, however, that the logical contradiction is not *immediately* evident. (I shall discuss this point in much more detail later on in this series.) He holds that some additional premises (or, perhaps, some quasi-logical rules which

---

[5]*Ibid.*, p. 47.
[6]*Ibid.*
[7]*Ibid.*
[8]*Ibid.*

2

will connect the terms "good," "omnipotent," and "evil")
must be recognized. The rules which Mackie suggests are:

> . . . that good is opposed to evil, in such a way
> that a good thing always eliminates evil as far as it
> can, and that there are no limits to what an omnipo-
> tent thing can do. From these it follows that a good
> omnipotent thing eliminates evil completely, and then
> the propositions that a good, omnipotent thing exists,
> and that evil exists, are incompatible.[9]

Mackie thus adds two premises to his original set of three:
(4) good is opposed to evil in such a way that a good thing
always eliminates evil as far as it can; and (5) there are no
limits to what an omnipotent thing can do. From these two
additional premises, Mackie deduces still another, (6) a good
omnipotent thing eliminates evil completely. From this array
of propositions, he then concludes that there is a logical in-
compatability between the following two propositions: (1) a
good, omnipotent thing exists; and (2) evil exists. By logical
incompatibility between these two propositions, Mackie means
that if one of the propositions is true, then the other must be
false. If a good, omnipotent thing exists, then, Mackie holds,
evil does not exist. On the other hand, if it is the case that
evil exists, then, he contends, that no good, omnipotent things
exist. Mackie further contends that since evil really does
exist, it is clear that no good, omnipotent thing (God) exists.

Significant to the effort to be made in this series of lectures
is the fact that Mackie admits: (1) that the logical contradiction which he claims is not *immediately* evident from his original three propositions; and (2) that his challenge to theism
(which is at least as old as Epicurus of the Third Century,
B.C.) can be defeated by setting out a position which adequately accounts for all of the vital factors involved in the
problem and which yet avoids inner contradiction. These ad-
missions are important because it follows (in Mackie's view)
that if anyone can set out positions which show how God

---

[9]*Ibid.*

could create (and yet evil occurs) without being morally blame-worthy, then Mackie's challenge will have been defeated. I shall discuss this matter in considerably more detail later in this series of lectures.

I. EPICURUS

In his essay on the wrath of God, Lactantius, a so-called Christian apologist of the fourth century, A.D., quotes Epicurus as follows,

> God either wishes to take away evils and is una-ble; or he is able and unwilling; or he is neither willing nor able, or he is both willing and able. If he is will-ing and unable, he is feeble, which is not in accord-ance with the character of god; if he is able and un-willing, he is envious, which is equally at variance with god; if he is neither willing nor able, he is both envious and feeble, and therefore, not god; if he is both willing and able, which is alone suitable to god, from what source then are evils? or why does he not remove them?[10]

In accord with Mackie, Epicurus deals with (1) the power of God; (2) the goodness of God, and (3) the existence of evils. Epicurus holds that these possibilities exist: (1) God is omnipotent but not omnibenevolent; (2) is omnibenevolent but not omnipotent; (3) God is neither omnipotent nor omni-benevolent; and (4) God is both omnipotent and omnibenev-olent. Epicurus holds that only (4), not (1), (2), and (3) is in accordance with the character of God. In other words, if what one calls God is not both omnipotent and omnibenevo-lent, then whatever it is, it is not God. Further, Epicurus im-plies (by the two questions at the end of the quotation I have just given) that if evil exists, then God cannot be both omnip-otent and omnibenevolent. So, he implies, since evil does exist, then God does not exist. It is clear that Epicurus bases

---

[10]Lactantius, "A Treatise on the Anger of God," in *The Ante-Ni-cene Fathers,* VII, ed. by Alexander Roberts and James Donalson (Grand Rapids: William B. Eerdmans Publishing Company, 1951), p. 271.

his argument on the view that there is logical incompatibility between these two propositions: (1) a good omnipotent thing exists; and (2) evil exists.

II. DAVID HUME AND HIS USE OF "EVIL"

In his *Dialogues Concerning Natural Religion*, David Hume makes two very important moves: (1) he contends that the affirmation that a good, omnipotent thing (God) exists and that evil exists involves a logical incompatibility; and (2) he argues that even if one were to grant that they are not logically incompatible, the theologian still faces the problem of major proportions in the existence of evil.

In making the first move, in Part X of the *Dialogues*, Hume has Philo ask, "Why have all men, I ask, in all ages, complained incessantly of the miseries of life?" Hume then has Philo, in the face of so much misery, to argue,

> His power we allow infinite: whatever he wills is executed: but neither man nor any other animal is happy: therefore he does not will their happiness. His wisdom is infinite: he is never mistaken in choosing the means to any end: but the course of nature tends not to human or animal felicity: therefore it is not established for that purpose. . . .
> Epicurus's old questions are yet unanswered.
> Is he willing to prevent evil, but not able? Then he is impotent. Is he able but not willing? Then he is malevolent. Is he both able and willing? Whence then is evil?[11]

In this statement, Hume has Philo arguing that theism (affirming that God is both omnipotent and omnibenevolent) involves a logical contradiction. If God were omnibenevolent, he would want to make all men truly happy. If he were omnipotent, he *could* make all men truly happy. Since men are *not happy*, then one of two things is the case: (1) God is ei-

[11]David Hume, "Dialogues Concerning Natural Religion," Parts X, XI in *God and Evil*, ed. by Nelson Pike (Englewood Cliffs: Prentice-Hall, Inc., 1964), pp. 17-36.

ther not omnipotent or not omnibenevolent; or (2) he is neither omnipotent nor omnibenevolent. Thus, Philo argues, God is either weak or ill-willed, or he is both weak and ill-willed. In any case, he is not an infinite God. If nature indeed shows the design from which Cleanthes (another of the characters in Hume's *Dialogues*) inferred the existence of God, why, Philo asks, does this marvelous design not extend to making people happy? Why, if a good, omnipotent God designed the world, does there exist any evil at all?

Demea, another character in Hume's dialogues, offers a counter-argument to Philo by saying that this world so filled with misery is merely a very brief preparation for life eternity. Since there will be no evils in eternity and since eternity will be so long in comparison to the few short years of life on earth, evil during one's earthly life is justified.

However, in a rebuttal to what seems to him to be a too easy escape, Cleanthes tries to prove that God is benevolent by denying that man is miserable and wicked. In the course of this effort, Cleanthes admits that if Philo can "prove mankind unhappy or corrupted" then there will be an end at once to all religion. He says, "The only method of supporting divine benevolence (and it is what I willingly embrace) is to deny absolutely the misery and wickedness of man."

In making the second major move, in the latter part of Part X and in Part XI, in reply to Cleanthes, Philo contends that even if he (Philo) were to grant Cleanthes's contention (which, he says, no one could ever prove) that human happiness in this life is greater than human misery, the existence of *any* evil at all would still be fatal to Cleanthes's affirmation that a good, omnipotent God exists. In pressing this point, Philo asks, "Why is there any evil at all in the world?" He then denies that the existence of evil can be rightly ascribed to mere chance. He holds that the misery of man must be due to some *cause*. What is this cause? he asks. Was it the intention of God? No, this cannot be the answer, for God is benevolent. Then was it something which was contrary to

God's intention? No, this cannot be the case, for God is omnipotent. He thus implies that the existence of evil proves that no perfectly good, omnipotent thing (God) exists, and he asserts that the only way one can escape the solidity of that reasoning is to admit that the entire subject is beyond the capacity of mere human beings and that man's "common measures of truth and falsehood are not applicable to it."

After having thus argued that the existence of an infinite God and the existence of evil are logically incompatible, Philo suddenly does what seems to be an about-face and says that he is willing to grant (perhaps merely for the sake of argument) that pain and misery in man are logically compatible with infinite power and goodness in the Deity. It seems clear that Philo is not making the concession because he now sees that his charge of logical incompatibility will not stand. Rather, he seems to be saying, in effect, "Cleanthes, even if I were to concede that no logical contradiction is involved, you would still face a problem of major proportions. If there is any evil in the world, you still cannot prove the existence of God." Hume has Philo to ask, "What are you advanced by all these concessions? A mere compatibility is not sufficient. You must prove these pure, unmixed, and uncontrollable attributes from the present mixed and confused phenomena and from these alone."

To understand Philo's point here, it must be noted that to Demea the existence of God is self-evident. With reference to that question, he says,

> No man; no man, at least, of common sense, I am persuaded, ever entertained a serious doubt with regard to a truth, so certain and self-evident. The question is not concerning the BEING, but the NATURE of God.[12]

He contends that the comprehension of the nature of God is beyond man. A theist of Demea's type (who holds that the

---

[12]*Ibid.*

existence of God is self-evident, *a priori*) affirms the existence of God and admits the existence of evil. From these two premises, it follows not that there *might* be a morally sufficient reason for the existence of evil, but that there *must* be such a reason. With such an approach, the only problem is that of ascertaining a specific theodicy (defense or justification of God) which is adequate to explain God's morally sufficient reason for allowing evil. And even this is not too important, for so long as one is convinced that there *is* such good reason, the specific reason becomes a matter of trivial importance.

But this is *not* the case with *Cleanthes*. He does not hold that the existence of God is self-evident. He does not offer an *a priori* argument. He argues from data which he encounters in the world. Specifically, he offers the design which he sees in the world as being the data which warrants his inferring that God exists. It is at this point that Philo makes his attack on Cleanthes. In effect, he says,

> All right, Cleanthes, suppose I admit that there is no logical incompatibility in affirming both that an infinite God exists and that evil exists, don't forget that your approach to the problem is to infer from the data which you find in the world that God exists. Please tell me how—when the world is the *only* data you claim—you can infer the existence of a God who is both omnipotent and omnibenevolent from a world which contains some evil, even if I grant that there is less evil than good? The truth of the matter is: the only conclusion you can rightly infer is that the source of the universe (whatever it may be) is indifferent to good and evil.[13]

Thus Philo contends that the existence of evil in the world should be recognized as evidence *against* the argument used by Cleanthes to infer the existence of God (the argument from design). Philo is saying that the existence of evil in the world offers evidence that Cleanthes's hypothesis is false, or at least is highly improbable.

[13]*Ibid.*

This effort of Hume on the problem of evil is used here to set out a basic *limitation* as to what I am trying to do in these lectures; that is, Hume's effort can be used to show what the problem of this discussion is *not*. From the *Dialogues,* two basic efforts of Hume have been noted: (1) he seeks to show that God and evil could not exist in the same world (this implies that the propositions "God exists" and "Evil exists" are logically incompatible): therefore, he concludes, since evil does exist, God does not exist; and (2) he seeks to show that even if Philo should grant (for the sake of argument) that no such logical incompatibility exists the theologian who depends upon *a posteriori* evidence (such as Cleanthes does in the use of argument from design) is still faced with a problem of major proportions. Hume seeks to show that this is the case because the only data from which the theologian can draw his inference (that a perfectly good, omnipotent being exists) is phenomena (in the world) which is a mixture of good and evil. Such data, Hume has Philo to argue, warrants the inference that the source of the universe is indifferent to good and evil, not that a perfectly good, omnipotent being (God) exists. In this series of lectures I will be concerned with the first basic effort of Hume and not with the second.

From the foregoing, the following seems to be clear: (1) the charge is made that Judeo-Christian (Biblical) theism involves a logical contradiction; (2) it is admitted that this incompatibility depends upon three propositions (supplied by Mackie) in addition to the three basic propositions which are involved in the affirmation of Biblical theism; and (3) it is admitted that the charge would prove to be false if anyone could set out a position which would adequately account for all of the vital factors in the problem without involving a logical incompatibility.

A PRELIMINARY LOOK AT HOW THE PROBLEM IS TO BE MET

According to J. L. Mackie, there are two basic ways by

which the problem can be met (or avoided): (1) one could deny at least one of the three basic propositions; and (2) one might explain the three basic propositions in such fashion as to hold on to all three while still avoiding the so-called problem of evil. Mackie holds that (1) is possible, but that (2) is impossible. I disagree with Mackie in ways I shall explicate as we go along.

According to Mackie, if one makes some sort of concession on at least one of the basic propositions, then he is no longer affirming traditional Biblical theism[14] and, Mackie goes on, if the theist does *not* make some concession, then, he cannot avoid the logical incompatibility with which Mackie charges theism.

Later in this series I shall talk about other ways of responding to the problems set out by Mackie. Quite obviously there is another way, (3), which has been overlooked by Mackie; viz., to show either that the "extra" propositions (quasi-logical rules introduced by Mackie and from which he deduces his basic conclusion) are false or that they have not been established by Mackie.

Since I myself am concerned with the *affirmation* of Biblical theism, way (1) as set out by Mackie is obviously not a tenable one for me. My effort, then, will be concerned with way (2). This is the case in spite of Mackie's contention that such is impossible. I will also be concerned with way (3).

---

[14] I agree with Mackie at this point; that is, that when a theist "gives ground" on one of the propositions which is basic to Christian faith, he is no longer a theist—at least he is not a Biblical theist.

Chapter II

J. L. Mackie's Basic Conclusion From The Fact of Evil and My Response To It

In this chapter, I shall: (1) consider in more detail (than in the previous chapter) Mackie's view of the incompatibility between theism and the existence of evil, (2) consider possible ways of responding to Mackie's argument, and (3) explicate in detail my own way of responding to Mackie's argument.

1. MACKIE'S VIEW SET OUT

From Mackie's statement regarding the existence of evil (quoted in preceding chapter) it will be recalled that he contends that there are three propositions which are basic to traditional theism. For the purpose of reference, I shall number these propositions and prefix an "M" to each respective number, thus distinguishing them from other propositions which will have the prefix "W." The prefix "W" will serve to indicate that such propositions have originated with *me* in *this* series of lectures. Mackie says that the three basic propositions are: M1: God is omnipotent, M2: God is perfect in goodness, M3: evil exists.

Of these propositions, Mackie says that the theist must adhere (in order to remain a Christian theist) but cannot *consistently* adhere to all three of these propositions, and that the conjunction of these three propositions results in a logical contradiction, so that, if any two of them were true then the third (remaining) one would be false.

However, Mackie admits that the logical contradiction is *not immediately* evident but *becomes* evident only when one brings into the picture some additional propositions (quasi-logical rules) which connect the terms "goodness," "omnipotence," and "evil." He thus develops two *additional* propositions: M4: Good is opposed to evil in such a way that a good thing always eliminates evil as far as it can, and M5: there are no limits to what an omnipotent thing can do.

But Mackie is not yet finished with his case. From these two additional propositions (M4 and M5), he *deduces* still another proposition, M6: a good, omnipotent thing eliminates evil *completely*.

Then, by a conjunction of propositions M1 and M2, Mackie states another traditional proposition, M7: a good omnipotent thing exists.

He completes his argument by contending, in what is the core of his entire argument, M8: there is a logical contradiction involved in the conjunction of propositions M7 (a good, omnipotent thing exists) and M3 (evil exists). As I have already noted, Mackie holds that if any two of the three basic propositions (M1, M2, M3) are regarded as true, then the remaining one must be regarded as false. This means that the conjunction of the three propositions results in a dilemmatic argument in the following shape:[15] If God *wills* the evil which exists, then he is not good, but, on the other hand, if he does *not* will it, (but it occurs anyway), then he is not omnipotent (he does not have enough *power* to prevent what he *wishes* to prevent). Since evil certainly *does* exist, then God either wills it or does not will it. Therefore, God is either not good or not omnipotent.

Put into symbolic terms (W = God wills evil, G = God is good, O = God is omnipotent), the dilemma looks like this (constructive dilemma):

[15]The basic argument is set out by R. G. Collingwood in his *Faith and Reason,* ed. by Lionel Rubinoff (Chicago: Quadrangle Books, 1968), p. 148.

(1) $(W \supset \sim G) \cdot (\sim W \supset \sim O)$

(2) $(W \lor \sim W)$

(3) $\therefore \sim G \lor \sim O$

This means, of course, that the theist is supposed to face the dilemma of choosing between: (1) it is false that God is good, and (2) it is false that God is omnipotent.

Since the argument is obviously valid, it can be shown to be unreliable only by showing that at least one of the premises is false. This I plan to do during this series.

Put into the form of a hypothetical syllogism, Mackie's argument looks like this:

(1) If *evil* exists, then *God* does *not* exist.

(2) Evil exists.

(3) Therefore, God does not exist.

Since the antecedent of the major premise is affirmed, the syllogism is unquestionably valid.   Thus, if the premises are true, then the conclusion *must* be true.   How, then, does Mackie attempt to prove the premises?   In connection with the major premise, he makes four distinct moves, which I here restate: (1) he claims that the conjunction of the three propositions involves a logical contradiction, (2) he introduces two additional propositions in order to make clear the contradictions, (3) he deduces another proposition from these two, and (4) he affirms that the conjunction of all these propositions makes the logical contradiction very clear.

Mackie makes no real effort to prove the minor premise (evil exists).   He seems to take the truth of that premise for granted.

Since I also grant that the minor premise is true, it is clear that the point of controversy is the claimed proof of the *major* premise. My effort in this series of lectures is designed to show that Mackie has *not* proved the major premise.

II. POSSIBLE WAYS OF RESPONDING TO MACKIE'S ARGUMENT

It is clear that Mackie is not claiming merely to have undermined the traditional arguments for the existence of God. Rather he is claiming that for one presently to be a Biblical theist, he must be prepared to believe not only what cannot be proved but what he, Mackie, has actually *disproved*. It would be difficult, if indeed not impossible, to imagine a stronger challenge or claim against Christian theism. How might Christian theists respond to such an imposing challenge? Let us look at some of the ways.

1. The Christian theist might just avoid the problem by pretending that there is no problem and simply ignoring it. Or, he might avoid the problem by calling it a "mystery," which is beyond man's intellectual capacity for solving. And, again, he might avoid the problem by denying that any evil exists. However, since the Bible plainly describes God as infinite, this course is not open to anyone who holds to Biblical theism.

2. The theist might attempt to "dissolve" the problem by denying that any empirical fact can count either for or against the view that God exists and resorting solely to the ontological argument to settle the problem of the existence of God.[16]

3. He could simply admit defeat as a Biblical theist. He could admit that Mackie has done what he (Mackie) claimed to have done; that is, that he has proved that God does not exist. Of course, when one makes such an admission, he is no longer a Biblical theist.

4. The theist might accept a weakened version of theism. He could do this by making a concession on, for example, one or more of the following propositions: God is infinite in

---

[16] As does Charles Hartshorne in his *Natural Theology*.

power, God is infinite goodness, God is infinite in knowledge and wisdom, or God is infinite in justice and holiness.

5. The believer in the God of the Bible might respond by attempting a philosophic proof of the existence of God. He could do this by using one or more of the traditional arguments. (Cosmological, teleological, or moral). If he were to be *unquestionably* successful in such an effort, it would be clear that Mackie's argument failed somehow or other. While I myself believe that such success can be attained, I shall not attempt such in these lectures.

6. The theist could respond to Mackie's argument by claiming some kind of *direct experience* with God; that is, he could claim that he had actually seen or heard God and that, therefore, no matter what Mackie may argue as to logical contradiction, his argument is simply false or unsound.

7. Or, in what is obviously the most appropriate way, the theist could set out to refute Mackie's claim and solve the problem. This seventh way will constitute my own basic response to Mackie's argument. In what follows I shall set out my own basic affirmation in regard to the argument made by Mackie relative to the problem of evil.

III. MY WAY OF RESPONDING TO MACKIE'S ARGUMENT—MY BASIC AFFIRMATION SET OUT

It will be recalled that Mackie contends that the problem of evil (in the sense in which he uses the phrase), is a problem only for those who believe there is a God who is infinite in both *power* and *goodness*. He insists that the problem is neither a *scientific* one (which might be solved by some decision, resolution, or action) but is a *logical* one. As to his claim that traditional theism involves a logical contradiction, he holds that there are two means by which it can be met or avoided. One of these ways (i.e., rejecting or denying at least one of the three basic propositions) I have already rejected. The other way (so explicating the basic propositions of theism as to show that the conjunction of such propositions does *not* necessarily involve a logical contradiction) I plan to accept and utilize in setting out my own basic affirmation.

1. *My basic affirmation (thesis) set out.* It is erroneous to conclude (as does Mackie) that the existence of evil in this world proves that the infinite God affirmed by Biblical theism does not exist, because: the concepts involved in the basic propositions of such theism can be so interpreted and so explicated as to avoid having to accept either a weakened version of theism, or the view that the conjunction of the basic propositions of theism necessarily involves a logical contradiction. This means that, since God has a morally justifiable reason for having created the world (that is, to be the ideal environment for "soul-making") in which evil can (and does) occur, the existence of evil in the world is not inconsistent with the existence of the infinite God of Biblical theism.

2. *The positive element of the basic affirmation set out.* The positive element of my basic affirmation is: The concepts involved in the basic propositions of Biblical theism *can* be so interpreted and so explicated as to avoid having to accept the view that the conjunction of the basic propositions of that theism necessarily involves a logical contradiction.

3. *The negative element of my basic affirmation is:* Mackie has *not* established his claim (to have proved that the infinite God of Biblical theism does *not* exist) by his affirmation that the conjunction of the basic proposition of Christian theism necessarily involves a logical contradiction. It is my plan to establish this element of my basic affirmation (thesis) by showing that at least some of the propositions crucial to Mackie's case are false (that is, to show them to be false in the course of establishing the positive element of my basic affirmation). All that is *necessary* to refute Mackie's claim is to show that *he* has not established the propositions which are crucial to his case. If he has not established the premises from which he draws his conclusion, then, as his argument

16

now stands, it is unsound. If I can show that one or more of the propositions upon which he builds his case is false, then I will have *definitely* shown that his argument is unsound.

IV. EXPLICATION OF MY BASIC AFFIRMATION

In the preceding paragraphs, I have briefly stated the problem as posed by Mackie. In doing so, I have pointed out that proposition M8 (affirming that the conjunction of propositions M7 and M3 involves a logical contradiction) is the very core of Mackie's challenge to Biblical theism. Since this is the case, and since it is clear that his establishing proposition M8 depends upon his prior establishing of additional propositions M4, M5, and M6, it is also clear that if one (or more) of these additional propositions can be shown to be false or even questionable (since Mackie claims that by his argument he has *disproved* the existence of an infinite God), then it will have been shown that Mackie has failed to make his case. In the course of explicating the positive element of my basic affirmation, I shall offer material which constitutes grounds for rejecting propositions M4, M5 (and thus, also, proposition M6—since the truthfulness of proposition M6 depends upon the truthfulness of both proposition M4 and M5). At this point, however, I wish only to point out the propositions with which I agree and those with which I disagree. Along with Mackie, I also *affirm* propositions M1, M2, M3, and M7. I *deny* propositions M4, M5, M6, and M8. In connection with the explication of the positive element of my own thesis, I shall set out some additional propositions.

I shall deny proposition M4 by contending that it is *not* the case that good is opposed to evil in such a way that a perfectly good thing (being) always eliminates evil as far as it (he) can. I shall deny proposition M5 by contending that it is *not* the case that there are no limits to what an omnipotent thing can do. I shall deny proposition M8 by arguing that since Mackie cannot prove propositions M4 and M5, proposition M6 (which Mackie deduces from M4 and M5) cannot be

17

regarded as having been established, for proposition M8 depends on proposition M6. This means, if I can show what I have indicated I shall attempt to show, that Mackie has not established that a logical contradiction is involved in the conjunction of propositions M7 and M3. When this has been acomplished, then Mackie's challenge to Biblical theism will have been overthrown.

It should be recalled that the logical contradiction (which Mackie claims to see) is *not immediately evident* from his original three basic propositions—and that thus his *conclusion* (as to logical contradiction) *depends upon* the *additional* propositions which he brings into the picture—and that Mackie's challenge to Biblical theism can be met by setting out a proposition which adequately accounts for all of the vital factors involved in the problem and which avoids inner contradiction. In the course of what I am now to do, I shall try to set out such a position. In doing so, I shall set out and explicate two elements of my own basic affirmation which is comprised of three elements: the positive element, the negative element, and the counter element. I shall defer a consideration of the counter element for another book because it is not vital to the problem at hand.

In the explication and defense of the specific propositions of Biblical theism to which I have already referred, I am especially concerned with upholding some ideas regarding God, man, evil, the world, natural calamities, animal pain, human suffering, and man's final destiny. It should be noted that these ideas are *crucial* to my basic affirmation. I will be concerned also with showing how each of these matters relates to my basic affirmation, showing in each case what limitations are applicable.

In regard to *God,* I shall be concerned to uphold the view that he exists and is intrinsically complete or perfect (that is, that I shall not "give ground" relative to any of his attributes) and that he is innocent of any blameworthiness in regard to evil or any other matter.

Although there will be no separate section devoted to the topic of *man* (this is the case because this topic will be discussed thoroughly in the sections on "God" and "sin" and because there will be a following section on man's final destiny), I shall be concerned to uphold the view that man is a free moral agent, that he is to be blamed for his own sins, that he is immortal, that his earthly life is his one and only probationary period, and that his fate in eternity will be determined by his response to God during his earthly life.

In regard to *the world*, I shall be concerned to uphold the view that it is as good (for the purpose God had in creating it) as any possible world, that it was designed to be a "vale of soul-making" for man, and that it was created in view of man's fall (into sin) which God (in his omniscience) knew would occur.

In regard to *evil,* I shall be concerned to uphold the view that nothing sub-human *is* or *can* be *intrinsicially* evil, that sin (that which contradicts sonship to God and brotherhood to man, that which violates the will of God and consists in loss of fellowship with God) is the *only intrinsic* evil, that only *man* —not God—is to be blamed for man's sins, that evil really does exist but that it is not evil that evil exists.

Later in the discussion I shall be concerned to show that such events as are involved in natural calamities, animal pain, and human suffering are *not* intrinsically evil. Rather, I shall maintain that they play a vital role in the world's being the ideal environment for "soul-making," and that such matters do not provide a proper basis for concluding that the God of the Bible does not exist.

I propose to establish the *positive element* of my thesis by using the procedure of "faith seeking understanding" and thereby do what Mackie himself admits would be an adequate refutation of his challenge; viz., to so interpret the concepts involved and, thus, to so explicate the propositions of Biblical theism, as to avoid any logical contradictions. My task will not be that of presenting a philosophic proof for each of these propositions, but will be that of showing, *granted* the elements of Christian faith, that the conjunction of the propositions thus explicated does not involve a logical contradiction. Mackie has claimed that this cannot be done and, thus, that all should acknowledge that the God of Christian theism does not exist. But if such an explication as I shall attempt can be accomplished, then Mackie's challenge (the basic problem of this series of lectures) will have been refuted. I plan in other works to present philosophic proofs of Biblical theism, but in this particular series of lectures, I shall be satisfied simply to show that Mackie has not proved atheism. I plan to show that he has *not* proved that God does not exist.

In just a moment, I shall set out or list the propositions of Biblical theism which are basic to the problem of evil. Because of certain advantages which come from so doing, I shall not discuss these propositions in the order in which I shall number them. Rather, I shall discuss them singly and in groups as it seems, in each case, to be most advantageous. Since the propositions seem (for the purposes of this discussion) to group themselves under the seven topics which I have already noted, I shall use these groups as a means of explicating the propositions. As each topic is discussed, the task will be to show how the respective propositions which comprise that topic relate to my basic affirmation (thesis).

Later on I shall also set out some matters which will serve as further clarification of the distinctions to be made between good and evil, between what is to be valued and what is to be disvalued. This will be a matter which is vital to this whole discussion.

V. LISTINGS OF THE PROPOSITIONS OF BIBLICAL THEISM WHICH ARE BASIC TO THE PROBLEM OF EVIL

Before thoroughly discussing these twenty-two propositions under the respective topic headings, I should like at this time to simply give a statement of them in the order of their numbering:

Proposition W1: God is omnipotent.

Proposition W2: God is perfect in goodness.

Proposition W2a: God is omniscient.

Proposition W2b: God is perfect in justice.

Proposition W3: Evil exists.

Proposition W3a: Sin (that which contradicts man's sonship to God and his brotherhood to man, that which contradicts the will of God as revealed in the Scriptures) is the *only intrinsic* evil.

Proposition W3b: It is not evil that there is evil.

Proposition W3c: Evil results in *every* case from an abuse of the free moral agency of man.

Proposition W4: It is *not* the case that good is opposed to evil in such a way that a good thing always eliminates evil as far as it can.

Proposition W5: It is *not* the case that there are no limits to what an omnipotent thing (being) can do.

Proposition W6: It is *not* the case that a good, omnipotent thing eliminates evil completely.

Proposition W7: A good, omnipotent thing exists.

Proposition W8: It is *not* the case that there is a logical contradiction in the conjunction of proposition W7 and proposition of W3.

Proposition W9: This world is as good as any possible world for the purpose God had in creating it (that is, to be the ideal environment for "soul-making").

Proposition W10: Every instance of human suffering results from some condition(s) which was necessary to providing man with the ideal environment of "soul-making."

Proposition W10a: God is not blameworthy for having created a world in which righteous and wicked persons suffer during earthly life.

Proposition W10b: God is not blameworthy for having

created a world in which there *seems* (to some people, at least) to be dysteleological suffering.

Proposition W11: Every instance of animal pain results from some condition(s) which was necessary to providing man with the ideal environment of "soul-making."

Proposition W12: Every instance of natural calamities (tornadoes, earthquakes, etc.) results from some condition(s) which was necessary to providing man with the ideal environment of "soul-making."

Proposition W13: Man's earthly life is a probationary period (that is, during which his fate in eternity is settled) and it is his *only* probationary period.

Proposition W14: Man is immortal (that is, man will live on after physical death in a non-probationary "period" which is non-ending).

Proposition W15: The "stakes" in eternity (the *blessings* of heaven and the *punishment* of hell) are of such magnitude as to render all suffering in this life of no ultimate negative significance.

Chapter III

My Basic Affirmation and The Attributes of God

As I have already explained, in regard to God, I shall be concerned to uphold the view that he exists and is intrinsically complete or perfect, that he is infinite in power, that he is infinite in love and goodness, that he is innocent of any blameworthiness, that he is infinite in knowledge and wisdom, and that he is infinite in justice (or righteousness).

I. PROPOSITION 2a: "GOD IS OMNISCIENT"

By affirming that God is omniscient (as this matter is crucial to the problem which I am discussing in this series of lectures), I mean to maintain that God knows whatever is *possible* to know. Specifically, I am concerned to affirm that he knows (what to man, at least, is) the future. More specifically, I am concerned to affirm the view that God knew that man would fall into sin before that sin actually occurred. Knowing that man would so fall, desiring to save man (because of his perfect love and mercy) from the just consequences of his own sins, knowing that man would need an environment in which to develop moral and spiritual character (and so come back to God, away from whom he had gone in his fall into sin), and having the knowledge of the environment needed by man (as his "vale of soul-making"), God created the world (which is as good as any possible world for its purpose) in which such things as earthquakes, tornadoes, disease, one animal eating another, and one man killing another, occur. God knew how to create a world which would provide for man an environment which was as good as any possible for the purpose of enabling man to be truly free and to have an environment in which he could best develop morally and spiritually. The Bible clearly teaches that God created *man,* created the *world* as a "vale of soul-making" for him, and planned for man's life on earth to be a probationary period which ends at the moment of his physical death (thus attaching vital significance not only to the world as a "vale of soul-making" but also to man's life in that world as the *only* time in which he can make the decision to turn to God in love, devotion, and obedience). The group of propositions which deal with the world as an ideal environment for man will also help to show how crucial to my basic affirmation is the view that God is omniscient.

II. PROPOSITION W2b: "GOD IS PERFECT IN JUSTICE"

The Bible clearly teaches that God is perfect in love and goodness, and I shall discuss in more detail this element of Biblical faith just a little later. However, we must note that while God is full of love for the *sinner,* he hates (has just and awful resentment against) the *sin* which the sinner commits. Both of these attributes (love of the sinner and hatred of the sin) have a place in the total character of God, and it must not be concluded that there is antagonism between them. Further, it must not be concluded that one can understand truly the character of God unless he understands not only God's hatred of sin but his love of the sinner as well.[17]

The Bible clearly teaches that God demands of his creatures that they be like him in moral character.[18] God himself is the ultimate, absolute good, and his will (as set out in the Scriptures) reflects that ultimate goodness. This point entails the view that he *enforces* (in the sense that he will

[17]John 3: 16; Romans 5: 8, 9.
[18]1 Peter 2: 21-25.

24

not merely *overlook* man's lack of love and man's disobedi-ence) the law which he has imposed, in harmony with his own perfect nature.

To affirm, as I certainly do, that God is *infinite,* is to af-firm that God is infinite in *all* his attributes. To be less than infinite in even one attribute, is to be less than God. Thus, he is infinite in power, in goodness and love, in knowledge and wisdom, and in justice. Further, being infinite in his nature, he cannot change in quality. This is clear for the following reasons: If he changed for the better, this would mean that prior to the change he was less good than after the change and so was less than infinite in the matter in which the change occurred. If he changed for the worse, this would mean that after the change he was less good than before the change and became less than infinite. Obviously, neither of these will do if God is infinite. Since this is the case, and since God is infinite in purity, if men are to be like God, they must be like God in spiritual and/or moral purity. To be *just* is to recognize and enforce this necessity. Since God is holy (perfectly good and just), he can fail to demand purity and to punish sin only by failing to be holy. And, to fail to be holy is to fail to be God. As perfectly good and loving, God intends only what is good for man. As perfectly just and righteous, he insists on what is fitting. To say that man is under obligation to do what God's law imposed upon him is also to say that God must demand that performance and must impose penalty when that demand is not met. To im-pose the proper penalty is the proper reaction of God's righ-teousness and justice (legislative and retributive holiness). No attribute of God can cancel out (or annul) another. His perfect integrity demands that he cannot lie; he cannot deny himself. His perfect holiness requires that he cannot view sin in a complacent fashion. His perfect justice requires that he cannot forgive the sinner without an atonement.

According to plain Bible teaching this atonement is found in Jesus Christ, the Son of God.[19]

I must make it clear, however, that to say that God inflicts or imposes proper penalties upon the sinner, is not to say that he is ever motivated by passionate selfish anger or caprice. Rather, the penalties which God imposes express the revulsion of his nature against all sin. With God all judgment is righteous; divine justice requires it for its own satisfaction. God is never guilty of either an improper love or an improper hatred; he loves what ought to be loved, and he hates what ought to be hated, as dictated by his own nature. If God lacked *hatred* for evil, he would lack real *love* for good. Only one thing could be worse than committing evil (sin): approval of or failure to hate and oppose evil. When the skeptic describes his own revulsion against the "evil" which he at least thinks he sees in the world, he should recognize that such is only a very small reflection of God's *perfect* hatred of every sin and of the revulsion of his perfect justice against every impurity and moral failure of his creatures.

Having created man as a free moral agent, God (as infinitely just) has the obligation of imposing proper penalties when men misuse the freedom which he has given them. To *do* less than this would be to *be* less than God.

III. PROPOSITIONS W1: "GOD IS OMNIPOTENT" AND W5: "IT IS NOT THE CASE THAT THERE ARE NO LIMITS TO WHAT AN OMNIPOTENT THING (BEING) CAN DO"

It should be noted that proposition W5 is the contradictory of proposition M5 (of Mackie) so that, if proposition W5 is established, proposition M5 will have been shown to be false. And, if proposition M5 is shown to be false, then Mackie's case against Biblical theism has been shown unsound.

---

[19]1 John 2: 1; 1 Timothy 2: 5; Hebrews 9: 11-10: 4.

By affirming that God is omnipotent (proposition W1), I wish to uphold the views: that God can do whatever is *possible* to be done (that is, he *can* accomplish whatever is subject to power), and that (in harmony with his perfection in goodness and in justice) he *will* do only what is in harmony with the absolute perfection of his own nature. By affirming proposition W5, I wish to hold that there are some things which simply *cannot* be done; i.e., some things simply are *not* subject to power—not even to *infinite* power!

To these two propositions it might be objected as follows:

It seems clear that to claim that God is omnipotent is to claim that there are *no* limits at all as to what He *can* do. Further, it seems clear that proposition W5 denies what proposition W1 affirms. To say that God is not infinite in power is to admit that He *is not* omnipotent, and to admit that there is even *one* thing which God cannot do is to admit that He is *limited* (and thus *not infinite* in power). Further, it seems clear to me that God is *not* infinite in power, for there are many things which He *cannot* do. Among the things that God cannot do are: He cannot make a rock so large that He cannot lift it; He cannot make a four-sided triangle; He cannot make a ball white all over and black all over at one and the same time; He cannot make a particular horse both be and not be at one and the same time. (An imagined objection.)

I find that the basic reply which John Hick gave to this sort of objection to be very helpful in replying to it. Rather than saying that God *cannot* do the things just referred to, it would be more in harmony with the truth to say simply that such things *cannot be done at all!* God is infinite in power, but power meaningfully relates only to what *can* be done, to what is *possible* of accomplishment—*not* to what is *impossible!* It is absurd to speak of any power (even infinite power) being able (having the power) to do what simply *cannot* be done. God *can* do whatever is *possible* to be done, but he *will* do only what is in harmony with *his* nature. Rather than saying that God *cannot* make a four-sided triangle, one would more accurately (or, perhaps, more meaningfully) say (in the light of the fact that the word "triangle" means a *three*-sided figure and cannot refer to any *four*-sided figure) that the making of four-sided triangles simply cannot be done. An objector, by saying, "Here is something which God *cannot* do, therefore, he is deficient or limited in power and is *not* omnipotent," implies that the making of four-sided triangles is something which God *could* do if only he had *more power*. It is clear that the implication is *false!* In the same way, it is absurd to say that God cannot make a ball which is at the same time both white all over and black all over. To affirm that a ball *can* be at the same time both white all over and black all over is to affirm a logical contradiction. It is to affirm an absurdity. Such a proposition does not really say anything at all. Rather than saying that God *cannot* do such (with the implication that he is *deficient* in *power,* so that if only he had *more* power he *could* do it), one should say that such simply *cannot be done*—that such is *not subject to power,* not even to *infinite* power! And so it is with all of the items mentioned above and with all similar points which might be conceived. I thus conclude that the fact that one can imagine logical absurdities (which *cannot* be accomplished) is *not* a telling blow against the view that God is infinite in power. Proposition W1 ("God is omnipotent") thus stands unassailed by this objection. Also, in what I have just been saying, I have elaborated proposition W5 ("It is *not* the case that there are no limits to what an omnipotent thing, Being, can do"). In doing so, I have shown proposition M5 ("There are no limits to what an omnipotent thing can do") to be false.

Since Mackie's entire case against Biblical theism depends upon his establishing proposition M6 ("a good, omnipotent thing eliminates evil completely"), and since establishing proposition M6 depends upon his establishing both proposition M4 and proposition M5, to have shown that proposition M5 is false is truly a significant move. Mackie's total argument involves the view that if God is omnipotent he could create free persons who are *guaranteed* (by God) against committing even one sin. Especially pertinent at this point is the contention of John Hick[20] (a contention which I accept) that there is a contradiction in holding that God made us so that we shall of *necessity* act in a certain way and that we are a genuinely independent person in relation to God. If it is the case that all of our thoughts and actions are predestined by God, then we are nothing more than helpless puppets in the sight of God, no matter how free and morally responsible we may *seem* to ourselves. A patient who is acting out a series of post-hypnotic suggestions might seem free to himself, but his decisions have already been decided by another will. In relation to the hypnotist, the patient is not a free person. So it is with man and his relation to God: it *is* possible for God to create puppets, but it is logically impossible for God to *guarantee* that his creatures who are free will *always* (i.e., without even one exception) freely choose to love and trust him. It is logically impossible for such beings to be created, and since this is the case, it is not a denial of the omnipotence of God to hold that men are, at times, guilty of failing to love, trust, and obey God.[21]

Let me say by way of summary that it is not a denial of the omnipotence of God to say that he *cannot* create a free moral agent who is *guaranteed* against even committting even one sin. It would be more accurate to say that the creation of such a being is impossible—that it does not lend itself to accomplishment, that it is not subject to power, not even to *infinite* power!

---

[20]*POR,* p. 42; *Evil and The God of Love* by John Hick (Harper and Row: New York, 1966), pp. 303-304.
[21]*POR,* p. 43.

IV. PROPOSITION W2, PROPOSITION W4, AND PROPOSITION W6

Proposition W2 says: "God is perfect in goodness." Proposition W4 says: "It is *not* the case that good is opposed to evil in such a way that a good thing *always* eliminates evil as far as it can." Proposition W6 says: "It is *not* the case that a good omnipotent thing eliminates evil *completely*."

It should be noted that proposition W4 is a *contradiction* of Mackie's proposition M4, and that proposition W6 is a contradiction of Mackie's proposition M6. When I have established propositions W4 and W6, I will have shown that propositions M4 and M5 (upon which Mackie's entire argument depends) are false. When I have shown that propositions M4 and M5 are false, I will have shown that Mackie's argument against Biblical theism is an unsound one.

To say that God is perfect is goodness (proposition W2) is to say that he would never plan or do anything out of harmony with his own *perfect* nature. It is to say that God *loves* all *good* and *hates* all *evil* (although, as I have already contended, he loves the *person* who commits the sin). His perfect justice, balancing with his perfect love, prevents his ultimately saving those who finally reject his love (who refuse to obey his will and thus become true sons of God). A God who was all love and mercy (to the exclusion of any consideration of justice and/or righteousness) would be unjust. But to be unjust is, in fact, not to be God at all. To affirm that an unjust being is God would be like saying that the water in a cup is really ice—only it is simply *unfrozen* ice!

But an objector to my basic affirmation (who accepts propositions M4 and M5, and who then deduces from them proposition M6) might well raise the following objection:

It is clear that no infinite God exists, for if he did, being infinite in both power and goodness, he would

30

not create a universe in which evil is permitted to occur and (posing a counter-factual hypothesis), if it ever did occur, he would immediately eliminate it completely. (An imagined objection)

This objection is a very general one and, in a sense, might be viewed as encompassing the whole of the problem. It is so general that all which will be said in this particular section which I am now discussing might be considered as comprising the total answer to it. However, at this point I am especially concerned with an explication and defense of proposition W6 and with a denial of proposition M6 (considering these two propositions in such fashion will require, of necessity, some overlap with the preceding explication of proposition of W3a). I wish to contend that God does not *permit* sin (the only real evil) in the sense which is crucial to the problem of evil (although I grant that one might contend that there is a sense of "permit" in which it might be said that God "permits" sin). This contention is made in the light of what the Biblical view of evil really is: "evil" is that which, according to God's will, ought not to occur or be. To be guilty of evil is to fail to function as a son of God or as a brother to man—in short, to be guilty of evil is to be in violation of the will of God. It should be recalled that I have already argued that acts which involve *only* physical objects (such as earthquakes, tornadoes, etc.) and/or non-human life (plants, insects, and animal life) do not involve *evil*. (Nothing sub-human can *fail* to function as a son of God or as a brother to man. This is the case because nothing sub-human has the capacity to become and/or live as sons of God or brothers to men.) With this view of evil, I am contending that God does *not* "permit" evil. The objection presently under consideration raises questions about the goodness and the power of God. If the theist insists that the *goodness* of God is infinite, the skeptic replies, "If so, then his *power* must be limited." If the theist asserts that God is infinite in *power,* then the skeptic replies, "If so, then

31

his *goodness* must be limited, and he is not morally perfect." By way of summary, let us note that the skeptic holds that if there really were a God, and if he really were infinite in power, then (since, in the skeptic's view, there is *nothing* which an omnipotent thing *cannot* do) it would be easy for him to *cause* pure (innocent moral) character to exist, and, if he were infinite in goodness, then he would *want* to cause or guarantee perfect innocence. Yet, the argument continues, he either *permits* it or it occurs *against* his will. If he *permits* it, then he is deficient in *goodness*. If it occurs *against* his will, then he is deficient in *power*. And, it may be the case (skeptics hold) that (if God exists) he may be deficient in *both* power and goodness. (The advocate of Biblical theism cannot accept a weakened version of theism and remain such an advocate.) In either case (deficient in either only one or in both of these attributes), he is not the infinite God about whom Biblical theists talk and write.

In reply to this objection, I deny the premise (affirmed by skeptics) that if God is infinite in power he could *prevent* all evil (sin) and, at the same time, cause all men to have perfect moral characters, never being guilty of sin on even one occasion. It should be recalled that I have already established that no concession (in the matter of limiting the power of God) is involved in the admission that some things are impossible of accomplishment. It is absurd to ask, "Why did not God *prevent* all evil (sin) and *cause* every man to have a perfectly pure character?" While it is true that such a question might be asked by those who hold that God has *permitted* (when he *could* have prevented) evil and could have *caused* (had he wished to do so) pure moral character to exist in every human being, it is nevertheless true that such a question is absurd. It is a contradiction to affirm that it is possible to create an intelligent, free moral agent and then place him in a situation in which he was beyond all *possibility* of sinning. No power, not even infinite power, can create a being who is a free moral agent and who is yet beyond even the possibility of sinning. This is the case because the possibility of evil is analytical to the definition of moral agency. Let it be supposed, for the sake of illustration, that God created man as a free moral agent but who *could not* sin. If he absolutely *could not* sin, what merit or virtue would there be in any given act of obedience or in the totality of his acts of obedience? Is it not the case that he really would not be a free moral agent at all? If so, then it is a logical contradiction to affirm that there can be a free moral agent who is beyond the possibility of sinning. It would be affirming both that X *is* free and X is *not* free. So, it seems clear that it is absurd to ask why God did not create free moral agents who are beyond even the possibility of sinning. Having created man free, God could not guarantee that he *remain* free from sin. If a man must be a free moral agent in order to *become* and to *live* as a son of God (in loving submission to) and as a brother to (in compassionate service to) man, then he must also be free to *refuse* to become and live as a son and a brother.

I have already made clear that the Bible teaches that the purpose of God in creating man was to have a being who (while having the power to choose to do otherwise) freely chose to believe in, to love, to obey—that is, to become a true son of God and a true brother to man. Certainly it is the case that God (because he is both omnipotent and omniscient) could have created beings who *looked like* (had the same physical *appearance as)* men who did not have the capability of ever making a wrong decision. But, if he did, such beings would be no more than mere puppets or robots. However, the Bible teaches that God wants men to recognize him as their Father, and that he wants them to be able to respond to him in *freedom*.[22] No moral and accountable agent can exist without such power. It seems clear that no power (not even *infinite* power) can create a moral and ac-

---

[22]Galatians 3: 26-4: 6; Matthew 11: 28-30

countable agent and withhold from it the power to choose to do evil or to secure it absolutely against the possibility of sinning.

It is, of course, the case that we can *imagine* that God creates a world in which every object in it is beyond the *possibility* of sinning. But, if one were to contend that such a world has moral and accountable agents in it, he would be contending for a contradiction, and absurdity. If he is willing to leave off his contention for free moral agents so that he may have a world free of both contradiction and evil, then he should recognize that his world, in being free of the possible of *evil,* is also free of the possibility of *good.* The objector can admit moral and accountable creatures into his world only at the expense of also admitting a logical contradiction. He can have it guarded against all possibility of *evil* only by making it impossible that any *good* should enter there. There is an absurdity involved in asking, "Why did not God make men who do not have the properties of men? Why did not God make man (a being with power to choose either to do good or to do evil) and withhold from him a basic property (attribute) of man (the power to choose either to do good or to do evil)?" It can be seen that the person who pursues this line of questioning is not (basically) asking, "Why did God create men and then *permit* them to sin?" but is (by implication) asking, "Why did God create man at all?" with the further implication that God is blameworthy for having created man.

Just at this point, I wish to raise the question, "Is it really the case that God has *permitted* man to sin?" As I indicated earlier, in one sense, it seems that one might contend that he has, for we assume he could have chosen *not* to create the world and man at all. If he had created nothing, then there could have been no evil. Further, if he had created the world but had not created beings with free moral agency, then there would have been no sin. In this very *broad* sense of "permit," it can be said that *God* made

34

it *possible* for sin to occur in his world. But it seems clear that such a broad use of "permit" is not very useful to the effort to find an adequate solution to the "problem of evil." So, I want to use "permit" in a more restricted sense. While we assume that God (had he *chosen* such a course of action) *could* have avoided creating man, once he *had* created him not even God (Infinite Power) could prevent man's sinning without infringing upon his nature as *man*. Not even *God* could give freedom of choice to man and then *guarantee* that it would *never* be misused even once. To say that God *permits* sin (in the sense in which I am here using "permit") would be to say that God *could* (if he *wished* to do so) *prevent* man's sinning without taking away from man a property (or attribute) which is essential to his being man (the freedom to choose either to do good or to do evil) but that he goes ahead and *allows* man to sin. God permits sin in the sense that he allows sin to happen, but he cannot prevent it, given the nature of the person (man) whom he willed and created. My point is: once man has been created, it is *not* the case that God could either *permit* or *prevent* man's sinning without so changing man's nature that he would no longer be *man* The view of some thinkers to the effect that God *could* save all men (if he *chose* to do so) but that, as a matter of fact, he arbitrarily *willed* to save only certain ones is pertinent here. This is the case because such a view entails the position that God could *prevent* man's sinning without infringing upon his freedom of will but that, as a matter of fact, God chooses not to *prevent* man's sinning but to *permit* such. I have already shown this view to be false.

At any rate, even if we should admit that God *permits* sin (in the "broad" sense to which I have already referred), the essential point is still maintained; God does not permit sin in the "narrow" sense of "permit." Also, it is clear that God does *not* in any away *encourage* or affirm sin. Thus, while we have not (as yet) considered the question as to whether God is blameworthy for having *created* man, we have disproved the contention that God is blameworthy because he made man with the freedom to sin. To plead for such a contention is, in fact, to plead that God should have created something (being) *instead* of man.

Thus, it seems clear that I have shown that proposition W6 is true and that proposition M6 is false: it is *not* the case that a good omnipotent Being always eliminates evil completely. Since Mackie's case depends upon proposition M6 being true, he has not established what he claims to have established: viz., that no *infinite God* exists. It is plausible to accept the view (as per Biblical faith) that a perfectly good omnipotent Being could have a morally sufficient reason for creating a total environment in which it is *possible* for evil to occur.

V. PROPOSITION W7 AND PROPOSITION W8

Proposition W7 says, "A good, omnipotent Being exists." Proposition W8 says, "It is *not* the case that there is a logical contradiction in the conjunction of proposition W7 and proposition W3."

Proposition W7 combines proposition W1 ("God is omnipotent") with proposition W2 ("God is perfect in goodness") and affirms existence of the conjunction. By stating that the Being who has both of these attributes actually exists, I do not obligate myself to present a philosophic proof of that existence—not in this series of lectures, at any rate. Rather, this again is a matter of "faith seeking understanding." Assuming that God really does exist and that he has both of these attributes (as clearly set out in the Bible), the task which I face here is that of showing that logical contradiction is not *necessarily* involved in affirming the existence of both God and evil (as Mackie claimed). My task here is that of refuting atheists—Mackie in particular.

Since propositions M8 (the contradictory of W8) depends upon the truthfulness of propositions M4, M5, and M6, and since it has been shown that these propositions have not been (and *cannot* be) established as true, it is clear that proposition M8 should be rejected and that proposition W8 should be accepted.

It should be noted that Mackie's challenge has been met: I have shown that he has *not* established his case! I have shown that some propositions which are crucial to his claim that no infinite God exists are false.

Crucial to my basic affirmation are the ideas of God which I have been discussing. If it could be shown that ground *must* be "given" on any of the attributes of God which I have been defending, then it would have to be admitted that Biblical theism cannot be established.

Chapter IV

My Basic Affirmation and Its Relation To Evil

The title of this chapter constitutes a very crucial point in this entire study. In discussing it, I shall be concerned to uphold the view that *sin* (disobedience to God's will as revealed in the Scriptures, that which contradicts sonship and brotherhood, that which involves the loss of fellowship with God) is the only real evil, that nothing subhuman is really evil, that man is responsible for his own sins, that evil (sin) really does exist, and that while it is the case that evil really does exist, it is not evil that it does exist. Also, in this particular section, I shall be concerned with making brief statements as to what is intrinsically good, what is intrinsically evil, what is instrumentally good, and what is instrumentally evil. In this connection, attention also will be given to such questions as: What is to be valued? What is to be disvalued? In this connection this section will anticipate some of the questions which will be crucial for the sections on natural calamities, animal pain, and human suffering. Some of the conclusions which I shall draw in this present discussion will be applicable to those matters to be considered later. In a later section, I shall set out a more detailed discussion as to the distinction between good and evil, between the valued and the disvalued.

The three propositions which are pertinent to the topic of *evil* are: proposition W3: "Evil exists," proposition W3a: "Sin (that which contradicts sonship and brotherhood) is the only intrinsic evil," proposition W3b: "It is not evil that

38

there is evil," and proposition W3c: "Evil results in every case from an abuse of the free moral agency of man."

Although there are many things (actions, events, states) which *seem* evil to some people, it is clear that, according to Bible teaching, sin is the only intrinsic evil.[23] Thus evil really does exist, for sin exists: men fail to do what they *ought* to do (i.e., *obey* God), and they do what they *ought not* to do (i.e., disobey God). At this point I would like to share with you a statement from Edwin Lewis,

> We have learned . . . that God is Father, therefore that God's expectation from men is for sonship and brotherhood. We may therefore say that, in the Christian view, sin is whatever is unfilial (contradicting sonship) and unfraternal (contradicting brotherhood). Not to be to God as a son, and not to be to other men as a brother—that is what Jesus described as sin.[24]

To that statement Lewis adds,

> This is not limited to actions: it reaches down into the inner life. Unfilial and unfraternal attitudes and states of mind are as sinful, that is, as un-Christlike, as unfilial and unfraternal deeds.[25]

While there is value to both of Lewis' statements, I should like to restate that sin is the transgression (violation of God's) law. I have already given proof of this fact.

The gas chambers of Belsen and Auschwitz were unforgettable proof, if such were needed, that men actually do what they ought *not* to do—they hate, insult, degrade, rob, inflict pain out of malice, murder, etc., all of which violate the will of God which is plainly set out in the Scriptures. Men thus sin; that is, their thoughts and deeds contradict both sonship to God and brotherhood to men. Such

---

[23]1 John 3: 4; Rom. 3: 19; 4: 15.

[24]Edwin Lewis, *Great Christian Teachings* (New York, Abingdon-Cokesbury Press, 1933), p. 32.

[25]*Ibid.*

thoughts and deeds are *intrinsically evil* and, thus, can never be right under *any* circumstance.

I also affirm that even though evil really does exist, it is not evil that such is the case. God created man as a free moral agent with the freedom to contradict sonship and brotherhood; that is, with the freedom to sin. Further, since man's freedom has been the "door" through which the only evil (sin) has come, then *man,* not God, is blameworthy for the sin which occurs.

Further, I deny that anything which occurs on the purely physical level (such as tornadoes, earthquakes, etc.) or on the *animal* level (such as an animal suffering pain or one animal killing and devouring another) is intrinsically evil. Rather, I affirm that *nothing subhuman* is intrinsically evil.

Neither pain nor suffering is intrinsically evil. Nothing that *merely* happens apart from some connection with a *will* can have moral predicates. Before the question, "Is pain an intrinsic evil?" can be answered properly, two further questions must be asked: "To whose *will* are you attributing it?" and "Is it in harmony with God's will?" (that is, does it contradict sonship or brotherhood, does it affect fellowship with God? Does it violate his will?). To say that a state, thought, or action is intrinsically evil is to say that some *will* brought it about and that it is out of harmony with God's will, that is, it is unfilial and unfraternal—in short, that it contradicts God's will as revealed in the Scriptures.

The mere fact that an action has resulted in *pain* is not sufficient ground to brand it as intrinsically evil. A *physician* is not evil (nor guilty of an evil action) when he inflicts pain in amputating a man's gangrenous foot. A *mother* is not evil (nor guilty of an evil action) when she spanks her small child for disobeying her in crossing a street which is heavily traveled. If pain *per se* were intrinsically evil, then *every* instance of pain (including those inflicted by kindly, skilled surgeons and by loving mothers) would be evil. Yet, such instances of inflicting pain are *not* evil. Why is this the case? It is the case because the *motives* and *actions* of those inflicting the pain in these cases were in harmony with the will of God. It seems clear, therefore, that no logical contradiction is involved in the infliction of pain by a perfectly good being. In fact, it seems that, at least in some circumstances, the inflicting of pain is the only thing which a good will could do.[26] Pain *per se* is neither intrinsically good nor intrinsically evil. "Evil" and "good" come into consideration only in relation to the will of the person who has brought the action or state about, and in relation to the will of God—that is, only in relation to the contradiction of sonship and brotherhood (and, thus, in contradiction to fellowship with God), that is, only in connection with the violation of God's will as revealed in the Scriptures.

Two basic propositions of Biblical theism are that God is perfectly good and that he is omnipotent. Must one reject at least one or the other of these when he admits that pain and suffering occur in the world? My basic affirmation answers negatively because, understanding Bible teaching regarding God's perfect goodness, men do not have to believe that God allows them to suffer through some defect in that goodness—that is, some defect in the goodness of God. Assuming that God is omnipotent, we do not have to believe that God allows men to suffer merely because he *cannot* prevent it. There is no compelling reason why men cannot believe that it is good for them to live in a world in which it is at least *possible* for pain and suffering (as well as *sin*) to occur. There is no logical contradiction involved in so believing. Men can even believe that the *possibility* of pain and suffering coming into their lives is a thing for which they *can* (and *ought* to) *thank* God.[27]

I therefore conclude that neither *pain* nor *suffering* is in-

---

[26]R. G. Collingwood, *op. cit.,* p. 155.

[27]See discussion of this point in explication of propositions W9, W10, and W11. Note: I am indebted to R. G. Collingwood for some of the thoughts expressed in this paragraph.

trinsically evil but that only *sin* (as I have already explained) is intrinsically evil. Anything else can, at worst, only *appear* to be evil—an illusion or a misconception—or can only be *instrumentally* evil. It is also possible to use the term "evil" to mean nothing more than that an object does not function as it was designed to do; e.g., one might say, "This is a bad (or evil) hammer," and mean nothing more than, "This hammer will not do what it was designed to do; namely, drive nails."

It should be noted also that while it is, in some cases, evil to *permit* evil when one can *prevent* it, it was not evil for God to create man with the freedom (of will) which enables him to do evil. To have created him without such freedom would have made of man nothing higher than a robot or a puppet. In such a case, man would not have been a moral being. But, once God had created man with freedom of will, he could not *prevent* (in the strict sense) his sinning without destroying man as man. It was not evil for God to create man with the *power* to do evil (sin) and to inflict pain and suffering, for such power is necessary for the power to do good. And, it is better that man should *be* than that he should *not* be. If this were not the case, it would be better if all men were simply annihilated.

Further, while it is true that God *is* responsible for there being the possibility for man to sin, God is *not* responsible for the *specific* sins committed by *individuals*. Since sin (that which violates the will of God) is the *only* intrinsic evil, there is *nothing* in the world for which God is *blameworthy*. And, since this is the case, Mackie has erred in concluding from the existence of sin and suffering that the infinite God of Biblical theism does not exist.

This particular matter would not be truly complete without more detailed attention being given to such questions as: What is intrinsically good? What is intrinsically evil? What is instrumentally good? What is instrumentally evil? What should be valued? What should be disvalued?

However, there is a sense in which every topic involved in this entire matter is concerned with such questions. Because this is the case, I shall use a separate section to discuss these questions in detail. This discussion—since it will be both a summary and a further elucidation—will follow the last of the seven topics which comprise the basic thesis.

Chapter V

My Basic Affirmation and The View That The World Is The Ideal Environment

Crucial to my discussion in this chapter is proposition W9 which says: "This world is the ideal (as good as any possible) world for the purpose God had in creating it (that is, to provide man with the ideal environment for soul-making)." In discussing this proposition, I wish to consider: God's purpose in creating the world, the characteristics a world should have in order for God's purpose to be realized, some suggestions (from skeptics) as to how the world might be improved, and what such suggestions imply.

I. GOD'S PURPOSE IN CREATING THE WORLD

Relevant to the explication of proposition W9 is the teaching of the Scriptures that prior to his creation of man and the world, God, because he is omniscient, had a plan. This plan involved the creation of a being (who would have descendents like himself) who would be capable of entering into fellowship with him, who would be capable of becoming a son of God, who (thus) would have to be capable of deciding freely to believe him, to love him with all of his heart, to submit to him in obedience, and whom God could love and eventually glorify. In the light of Bible teaching, we conclude that this is basically the one purpose which God had in creating the world. Because God is infinite in knowledge, he foresaw (if such is proper language in referring to God, who transcends time) that in order to have such a being, that being (man) would have to live in an environment which was ideally suited for the accomplishment of this purpose. What characteristics would or should such a world have?

II. CHARACTERISTICS OF THE IDEAL ENVIRONMENT

At this point in the discussion, I wish merely to set out the essential characteristics of such a world. Explication of *some* of these characteristics will follow in this section, while explication of those characteristics not fully discussed in this section will be discussed in following sections. This means that the explication of even those sections which deal with natural calamities, animal pain, and human suffering will be relevant to my affirmation that this world is as good as any possible world for the purpose which God had in creating it.

What would be the characteristics of a world which is designed to be man's ideal "vale of soul-making?" It must not be concluded that such a world would be merely a hedonic paradise in which man could experience *pleasure* but *not pain* (or, for that matter, adversity of *any* kind). The ideal environment would surely be one which allowed man to be a *free moral agent* (thus providing an "epistemic distance" between man and God). It would *reveal* God to man without *overwhelming* man, so that he is not really free. Yet, it would not necessitate a "gap" so large that man *could* not be drawn to God. It would be one which was both law-abiding and teleological[28] (one which was designed for this specific purpose and upon which man could depend for *regularity* of response). The ideal environment for man would be one which provided for his basic physical needs: air, water, food, clothing, shelter, medicinal supplies, etc. It would have to allow man the possibility of *challenging* his intellectual

_____
[28]Cf.: Stuart Hackett, *The Resurrection of Theism* (Chicago: Moody Press, 1957), pp. 354-356.

powers and of thus gaining knowledge. It must offer man the challenge of overcoming something (obstacles) in his environment.

It must be an environment which offers to man the *challenges* of choosing to become and to live as a son (of God) and a brother (to one's fellow-man) at a possible very high price (a great deal of sacrifice). In the face of the fact that it would allow the occurrence of various forms of adversity, it would supply, not a detailed explanation of each and every incident which might occur, but a sort of "supreme instance" by which all lesser events might be interpreted properly. It would thus allow man (if he reacted properly) to rejoice in the various forms of adversity or tribulation. Just a little later I shall say more about God giving man a "supreme instance" by which man can judge all lesser events.[29]

The ideal environment would be one in which the things which occur (other than the decision to become and live as a son of God and as a brother to man) are insignificant in comparison with the issues of eternity. Yet, even though it must be an environment which, since it is God's purpose to glorify man eternally, is a *temporary* one, it must also be one which is *highly significant* (ultimately crucial); i.e., it must be one upon which something turns which is of the greatest possible *importance* to *man*.

In connection with the foregoing claims as to the ideal environment for man, at least these questions arise: Are these the characteristics of an ideal environment? If yes, how can we more simply *classify* these characteristics? Does our present world possess these characteristics? If not, what additions, subtractions, or modifications might be suggested as improvements? And what are the implications of pleading for a modified world?

In answer to the first question, I reply, "Yes, these are

---

[29]Cf. Romans 8: 32; John 3: 16.

the characteristics of the ideal environment for soul-making." In reply to the second question, I reply, "Yes, these are the characteristics of our present world."

In just a moment, I shall explain *why* I thus answer these questions, and consider why the claims for an improved world do not overthrow my position.

Before doing so, however, I should like for us to note a way the characteristics of the ideal environment for soul-making might be classified. The ideal environment for man must be one which: supplies man's basic *physical* needs, allows man to be a *free* moral agent, allows man to *be challenged,* and allows man *to learn* the things which he needs most to learn. These characteristics will be discussed at some length in this present section, a little further in the section on natural calamities and in the section on animal pain, and, in greatest detail, in the section on human suffering.

The necessity of the characteristic first listed above is quite obvious. Since man has a physical body, in order for him to live, his environment must make available certain basic needs such as air, water, food, clothing, etc. As to the next characteristic which I have set out, we know (from Bible teaching) that God foresaw that man would need an environment in which to live while he made his decision to either accept or reject sonship (in relation to God). God further saw that in order for man's decision to be truly meaningful, his decision would have to be made freely. Further, in order for man to be free, he would have to live in an environment in which there was neither an overwhelming "tug" (persuasion) in the direction *toward* God nor one in the direction *away from* God. Two extreme situations would have to be avoided: a situation in which man lived *directly* in the *presence* of God, and a situation in which he did not have an adequate manifestation (or evidence) of God's existence. The environment which man needed would have to be one in which man would be at an "epistemic distance"[30] from God yet not so far away as to preclude his freely making his own decision to come to God in love and submission (to live truly as a son of God). This means that for man to be truly free in relation to God, his environment must be one which makes it *possible* for man to consider the world without immediately and automatically deducing the existence of God from that consideration. Yet, at the same time, we assume that it must be an environment from which it is possible to deduce correctly that God does exist. For one man, the world may *veil* God; for another man it may *reveal* him. This is as it *must* be—if man is to be truly free. He can feel the "tug" to choose *the world* by (becoming *self*-centered) rather than the "tug" to choose *God* (by becoming *God*-centered—and, to some lesser extent, brother-centered). At the same time, however, he lives in a world which declares (to him who will *allow* himself to see it) the glory of God.[31] This declaration is at least part of the "tug" in the direction *toward* God. Since God is infinite in power, knowledge, and goodness (and thus will *never* make a choice for the "second best" of anything), we assume that no better world (for the purpose God had in creating it) could have been created. And, there is nothing in the nature of things which compels us to believe otherwise.

Foreseeing man's fall into sin, because God is perfect in *justice,* (and thus, we assume, could not simply *overlook* sin), because he is perfect in *love* and *goodness* (and thus did not wish even one man to be lost[32]), and because he is perfect in *knowledge* and *wisdom* (and thus could plan the very *best* thing to do in the situation), the Bible teaches that God planned a way out (a scheme of redemption) for man.[33] There is a sense in which we might assume that God

---

[30]As Hick argued, *Evil and God of Love,* pp. 316-317.
[31]Romans 1: 18-32; Psalm 19: 1.
[32]2 Peter 3: 9.
[33]1 Peter 1: 18ff.

planned a scheme of redemption for man and, in a sense, planned man for the scheme of redemption—that is, man was planned to be a creature who *could* be involved in a scheme of redemption which depended upon man's *free* decision and upon man's having the intellectual, moral, and spiritual capacity to be involved in such a scheme. It was not the case that God arbitrarily selected certain ones to be saved (from sin and its consequences) and others to be lost.[34] A God who would set up a plan involving such arbitrariness would be deficient in goodness (and perhaps also in wisdom and power). Such a God would not be worthy of man's worship. It must be noted that the basic ground of the atheist's objection to traditional theism is that God both *could* and *should* have made a *better world* than the one in which we live. But this contention raises the question, "Better for what purpose?" What the atheist is here contending for is a sort of hedonic paradise in which pain, suffering, and sin do not occur. Mr. McTaggart put it this way:

> We come now to the relation of omnipotence to goodness. There is evil in the universe. It is not necessary to inquire how great or how small the amount of evil may be. All that is important for the present discussion is that there is some evil, and this is beyond doubt.[35]

A world in which it was absolutely *guaranteed* that not even one instance of "evil" could occur, would be unacceptable as a "vale of soul-making" for at least these reasons: it is impossible to have free moral agents in such an environment; given his freedom, man needs a *challenging* environment in order to *make* moral and spiritual decisions during his probationary period; and man needs such an environment in order to be able to *develop morally* and *spiritually*.

---

[34]Mark 16: 15, 16; Matthew 28: 18-20; Acts 10: 34, 35.

[35]J. M. E. McTaggart, "God, Evil, and Immortality," in *Religion from Tolstoy to Camus,* ed. by Walter Kaufmann (New York: Harper and Row, Publishers, 1961), p. 455.

The Bible teaches that the presence of pleasure and the absence of pain are not the supreme ends for which the world was created.[36] The value of the world is not to be decided upon the basis of the quantity of pleasure and pain which occur in it at any particular moment. Rather, it is to be decided upon the basis of its fitness as the ideal environment in which man can decide whether to become a (spiritual) son of God and a (spiritual) brother to his fellow-man. Since God's aim was to bring men to eternal glory,[37] I conclude that the kind of world he has created was determined by what would be the best instrument for accomplishing that aim. It was not God's intention to provide man with a hedonistic paradise but with the environment which is best suited for the moral and spiritual *development* of *man* toward the perfect pattern which is Jesus Christ. The world in which we live is as good as any world *could be* for that purpose. It is the world in which one can best live as a *free* and *responsible* person (one who can respond freely to God in love and devotion or who can reject God and still be responsible for whatever decision is made).

III. OBJECTION A CRITIC MIGHT RAISE

It might be objected (by an atheist) that our world is *not* as good as any possible world because it can be *improved*. In considering this objection, I want to analyze the objection and to set out how I plan to reply to it.

In analyzing the objection, first I want to raise two questions: Since you (the atheist) are claiming that our world can be improved, are you claiming that it can be improved as an environment for "soul-making"? If so, which characteristics of our world, if changed, would make our world a better "vale of soul-making"?

Perhaps an atheist would reply that our world would be "better" than it now is: if no natural *calamities* (such as

---

[36]See the Book of Job; 2 Corinthians 5, 12; Hebrews 12.
[37]John 10: 10; 1 John 2: 25; Titus 1: 2.

50

earthquakes, tornadoes, etc.) ever occurred; if there were no instances of animal pain; if there were no instances of *human suffering;* and if there were no instances of *sin.*

IV. IMPLICATIONS OF THE OBJECTION

I have already discussed the matter of *sin,* showing that not even God (with *infinite* knowledge, goodness, power, and justice) could *guarantee* that no *sin* could ever occur (although, *ideally* it is not his will that even one sin should occur[38]) if there are to be truly *free* beings.

Just a little later I shall discuss in detail the specific matters of: natural calamities, animal pain, and human sufferings. In doing so, I shall explicate in considerably greater detail the remaining (i.e., not already explicated) characteristics of our world which make it as good as any possible world.

Before addressing myself to those tasks, I wish to say a word about the *principle* involved in the possible objections which I have just noted. The principle upon which such objections (actually, it is only *one* basic type of objection) are made is that of "pulling the thorn from the paw of the limping world."[39] What this principle says, in effect, is that the things men hold to be wrong with the world are like *thorns* in the paw of an animal. All one needs to do to *correct* or, at least, *improve* the situation (the objector's argument goes) is to extract the "thorn" (specific evils in the world) and the "animal" (the world) will be "well" (the best of all possible worlds—or at least *improved* over what it is *presently).* But "correcting" the ills of the world (such as ridding it of all tornadoes, pain of animals, and pain of children) is not as simple an affair as some would have us believe—it is much more like a surgical operation in which the *entire* nervous system (which enables the animal to experience pain)

---

[38]1 John 2: 1.

[39]An illustration used by Austin Farrer in his book, *Love Almighty and Ills Unlimited.*

51

is extracted than it is like pulling only one thorn out of a single paw.[40] This is the case because it is impossible to "extract" a single "evil" from the totality of the world and not affect any other of the constituent elements of the total situation which is the world. It is easy to say, "Just remove from the world all animal and infant pain, and the world will be better than it now is," but it is much harder to explain just how radically *other* constituent elements of the world will have to be changed (extracted or substituted for) in order to bring about a total world in which no animal pain or infant pain occurs. One simply cannot extract animal pain from the world without *changing the nature* of either the animals or the world or both. Exactly what changes would be made? Would the *animals* be so altered that they could no longer *feel* anything (especially, that they would not feel pain)? Would the physical *environment* of the animals have to be so changed that when one runs into some object (such as a tree or a rock) *the object* does not hurt (because it suddenly turns into some sort of soft mush or air)? Would the situation be one in which no man or animal ever runs injuriously into things? The objection thus implied might take one of two forms. First, one could argue that God, being omnipotent, could so change the nature of the *world* that it would no longer be a law-abiding one and claim that if an animal were about to run into a tree he could miraculously dissolve the tree so that the animal would not be injured. Or, second, one might argue that the world would still be a law-abiding one but that the *laws* themselves would be changed in such fashion that animals are not injured when they "break" those laws.

Since the *first* form of the objection implies the view that the *world* would be so changed that it would no longer be a law-abiding one, it must be remembered that moral experi-

---

[40]As Farrer well argues.

ence cannot occur in a chaotic environment. And, if there is no lawful relation between action and reaction, then there is chaos. Stuart Hackett well says:

> Moral experience depends . . . upon rationality, since morality is, in the final analysis, the rational conduct of life: but the rational conduct of life would be impossible in a world not sustained by regular laws and explicable in causal terms.[41]

Since, according to this argument, a law-abiding world is the necessary environment for the making of moral and spiritual decisions and for moral and spiritual progress, if our world were to be changed so drastically as to change it from a law-abiding world to a non-abiding one, it would no longer be *ideal* as a "vale of soul-making." As F. R. Tennant well argued, if man's environment were not characterized by law or uniformity (regularity), man could not even "employ his reason in the conduct of his life. And, without rationality, morality is impossibile."[42] It would follow, from this line of reasoning, that since a universe of law is the necessary instrument of God's ultimate moral purpose, such a universe (with the inevitability of pain consequent to broken laws) is justified in its existence.[43]

The second form of this objection denies that *improving* the world (by eliminating animal and human pain) would result necessarily in a non-law-abiding world. Rather, it would hold that the world would still be characterized by physical *laws* but that the laws would be different from what they now are. However, this view raises the question as to whether such laws could sustain animal life. This is the case because of the value of pain in causing an animal to cease (or at least greatly diminish) its activity after it has been injured. Further, such a view would necessitate

---

[41]Hackett, *op. cit.,* p. 354.

[42]F. R. Tennant, *Philosophical Theology,* II (Cambridge: Cambridge University Press, 1930), pp. 199-200.

[43]Cf.: Hackett, *op. cit.,* p. 356.

"laws" which are so odd (peculiar) that various items in the world would be forced to have at one time a certain property and not to have that property at another time. For example, if a man were dying of thirst, water would have to have the properties which it now has, but if a man who could not swim fell into a lake, in order for the man not to drown, water suddenly would have to take on another (different) set of properties. Or, if a man were using an axe on a *tree* it would have the cutting power which an axe now has in our present world, but if one man were to try to use an axe on an animal or another man then the axe would have to lose its property of being able to cut through a man's body. It might be questioned whether such "laws" are really law. At any rate, it seems clear that such a sitation would be really only another form of chaos, and a world characterized by such conditions hardly would be an ideal environment for such moral decision and development. What rational man would argue for such chaos to be characteristic of man's environment?

It seems that when we arrive at the description of a world in which man could best live as a free and responsible person, that that description fits the world we presently live in: it is one which *provides* man's basic needs, it is *teleological* (created by God for the purpose of being a "vale of soul-making" for man); it is *law-abiding* (not chaotic and arbitrary), which it must be if it is to provide an environment for a rational, moral response by man (thus allowing the *possibility* of sin, pain, and suffering); it is *challenging* (allowing man to choose *suffering* over sin); and it is one which allows man to *learn* the things which he needs most to learn (including the possibility that man can learn the will of God[44]).

From the foregoing, I conclude that the skeptic cannot marshall evidence from any constituent element(s) of the world

[44]John 8: 32.

from which to deduce the conclusion that God is blame-worthy (for having produced such a world) and thus not perfect in goodness. And I conclude that this present world is as good as any possible world (for the purpose God had in creating it) and that, thus, God is not blameworthy for the evil and suffering which occurs in it. Apart from the view that the world was designed by God as the "vale of soul-making" for man, I do not see that the pain, suffering, and sin which occurs in the world could be justified.

Closely related to the topic of this section are the topics to be considered in following sections: natural calamities, animal pain, human pain and suffering, and man's final destiny. Some of the characteristics of the ideal environment (for "soul-making") will be explicated further in these following sections. Also, it should be noted that the material in this present section (in explication of proposition W9) is vital to the explication of the propositions which deal with natural calamities, animal pain, and human suffering.

Chapter VI

My Basic Affirmation (Thesis) and
Natural Calamities

Before stating and explicating the single proposition involved in this section, I should like to note that this and the following two sections deal respectively with natural calamities, animal pain, and human suffering. It might be the case that an objector would ask, "Since you have contended that sin (that which is contrary to sonship of God and brotherhood of man—that which is a violation of God's will as revealed in the Scriptures) is the *only* evil, why are you concerned at all with such matters as natural calamities, animal pain, and human suffering?" I offer three grounds for considering these matters.

First, I consider them because some thinkers claim that there are conditions (animal pain, etc.) in the world which God (if, they continue, he exists at all and if he created the world) has made which are evil, and which thus prove either that God does not exist or that, if he does exist, he is deficient in either goodness or power or both. In explicating my propositions on natural calamities, animal pain, and human suffering, I show that such is not the case.

Second, I consider such matters because some thinkers demand such a treatment. They hold that any claimed solution to the problem of evil which does not take such matters into account is wholly inadequate. This contention takes a form something like this, "If you say that animal pain and human suffering are not *evil*, then I say, call animal pain or human suffering 'X'—and it is *still* a problem for me. It still seems to me that if there were an infinite God, he would not have made a world in which animals kill and devour one another and in which human beings die horrible, lingering deaths from such diseases as cancer." In considering these matters, I show how they fit into the totality of the world as a "vale of soul-making."

Third, closely akin to the first and second grounds for considering these matters, I point out that I need to show that the total situation (of the world) is one which is ideal as an environment in which man can freely accept or reject God's invitation to become and live as a son of God and as a brother to man—that is, in harmony with God's will as revealed in the Scriptures. God's purpose in creating the world is thus a justification of the possibility of natural calamities, animal pain, and human suffering.

Proposition W12 is the only proposition involved in this present section. That proposition says, "Every instance of a natural calamity results from some condition(s) which was necessary to God's providing man with the ideal environment for 'soul-making.'" It should be recalled that the explication of proposition W9 (affirming that this present world is as good as any possible world, for the purpose God had in creating it) is highly relevant to proposition W12, and the discussion of proposition W12 should be considered in the light of that explication.

This is the case because in explicating proposition W9, I have affirmed that to be the ideal environment for soul-making our world must be characterized by law or regularity of response and be of such nature as to allow man to learn something of its conditions of response. I have further affirmed previously that nothing sub-human is intrinsically evil; only a being with the capacity to be both a son to God and a brother to man and to do that which contradicts sonship and brotherhood can be guilty of that which is intrinsically evil. I thus conclude that such objects as trees, water, wind, mountains, deserts, shifting of the earth, rain, etc.—or even dogs, cats, tigers, lions, leopards, and snakes, etc.—cannot be evil *per se* or be guilty of evil.

If the critic objects by saying,

> Even if I were to grant that, in order for there to be a *physical* world, there must be the *possibility* of the occurrence of mutual-interferences or cross-accidents, it nevertheless seems clear to me that there is no need for such *violent* ones as tornadoes, hurricanes, earthquakes, floods, etc. What contribution does an earthquake which destroys twenty thousand people (including many infants) make to 'soul-saving'? (An imagined objection.)

It is to be doubted that any man has (or *could* have) the knowledge to explain completely the contribution (to "soul-making") of every instance of such destructive forces. Nevertheless, it seems clear to me that God is not blameworthy for having created a world in which such events occur. This is the case because God has a morally justifiable reason for having created such a world. This means that it is possible to set out an explanation which is consistent with the basic propositions which are crucial, so far as the *problem of evil* is concerned, for Biblical theism so that such instances of destruction need not be assumed to support necessarily a case opposed to my own arguments.

It must be remembered that God did not create the world to be man's permanent home but to be merely his temporary "vale of soul-making," the environment in which man's one and only probationary period is to be spent. In that connection, it is good for man to realize that his life on earth will be brief (i.e., it is certain that his life on earth will *end),* and that the exact time of that end is uncertain. Such natural calamities as noted above are of such nature as to provide man with reminders of these two important facts. This is not to say that such events *force* (in the sense of *overwhelming* so that there is no alternate choice) man to the acceptance of these views. But, they afford *conclusive evidence* for such, provided one will use properly his own free will. The realization that one's life on earth is both *certain* (as to the fact that it *will* end) and *uncertain* (as to the exact time that end will occur) should lead men to give most serious thought to the questions of God and the proper response to him. The destructive power and the uncertainty of such events should serve as a reminder to man that this world is not his permanent home. This, too, could play a vital role in an environment designed for "soul-making."

The element of uncertainty as to the *persons* who will suffer some loss from such events can also play an important role in "soul-making." If one could be certain that he could avoid all such calamities by becoming a son of God (and living in submission to his will), this certainty could be a great obstacle to one's deciding to love and to submit to God from the proper motive (thus becoming a true son of God). It is not the case that God wants man merely to do action X, action Y, and action Z. He wants them to do those actions because of *love* for him—no matter how great a price might have to be paid for such obedience. God would have men to choose suffering over sin.[45] So, the uncertainty as to what *persons* (infants, righteous men, wicked men) will be struck by such calamities can be a vital constituent element in the total situation which is man's environment for "soul-making," his *temporary* environment, not his *permanent* home.

---

[45]Hebrews 11: 24-26; Revelation 2: 10; Luke 14: 26-33.

Chapter VII

My Basic Affirmation and Animal Pain

The only proposition which I shall discuss in this chapter is proposition W11, which says, "Every instance of animal pain results from some condition(s) which was necessary to God's providing man with the ideal environment for 'soul-making.'" In this chapter, I shall set out an objector's approach to and use of this element of the problem, make a brief statement of what has been said on this point in preceding chapters, state the basic questions involved, answer those basic questions by explicating proposition W11, and draw some conclusions.

I. AN OBJECTOR'S APPROACH TO THE PROBLEM OF ANIMAL PAIN

It seems clear that an objector's approach to the problem of animal pain is based upon a previous rejection of the view that there can be a higher purpose to man than can be fulfilled during his earthly life.[46] If this rejection be granted, then it also seems clear that animal pain cannot be made to seem plausible. But in proposition W11, I reject this position, holding that every instance of animal pain bears some relation to the view that there *is* a higher purpose for man than can be fulfilled in this life. This is made clear by plain Bible teaching.[47]

---

[46]Compare: Nels F. S. Ferré, *Evil and the Christian Faith* (New York: Harper and Brothers, Publishers, 1947), p. 57.

[47]Hebrews 9: 27; 2 Corinthians 5: 1-11; Titus 1: 2.

II. WHAT HAS BEEN SAID ON THIS ELEMENT
IN PRECEDING CHAPTERS

It will be recalled that I have already argued that this world cannot be improved as an environment for "soul-making" by: *adding* something which is not presently a constituent element of this world, *subtracting* something which already is a constituent element, or *modifying* something which is already an element of this world. To do what would be necessary to rid completely the world of animal pain would be such a *drastic* operation as to render the world unsuited as an environment for moral and spiritual decision and development. This is the case because such an alteration would be much more like removing the entire nervous system from an animal than it would be like removing a thorn from its paw.

III. SOME BASIC QUESTIONS ARISE

From the foregoing, a few basic questions arise: Why, if there must be animals, must they endure pain? Why are there any animals at all? If to have animals necessitates their experiencing pain, would it not be better if there were no animals at all?

IV. THESE BASIC QUESTIONS CONSIDERED

The first question is related closely to the argument set out in my remarks just preceding. The world would have to be altered greatly if it is to be one in which it is absolutely *impossible* for an animal to experience pain. The animal could not have a *physical* body if it is to be *impossible* for it to experience pain. Or, if it *is* to have a physical body, it would have to be a physical body *without* a *nervous system* (so that it could never *experience* pain). But such a creature would not know when to eat food (since it could not experience hunger pangs), when it should drink water (since it could not experience thirst), when it should stop running or digging following an injury (since it could feel

61

no pain from the injury), when it should tend to elimination of wastes from its body (since it could not feel the need to do so), etc. These facts are insurmountable difficulties to the total view implied by the objections set out above. In a word, pain serves a useful function, as I have already explained in some detail. Pain has a special value to the animal itself in that it serves as a warning that something has gone wrong (has been injured or has become diseased) with the animal's body. In this capacity, pain influences the animal to avoid doing things which would be harmful to it, and also to rest (immobilize) its body during times when activity would not allow some part of its body to heal. In reply to the second question, I shall explicate proposition W11.

V. EXPLICATION OF PROPOSITION W11

In connection with the second question which I have just set forth, (implying that it might be better if there were simply no animals at all), I reply by explicating proposition W11: "Every instance of animal pain results from some condition(s) which was necessary for man to have an ideal environment for 'soul-making.' "

Animals experience pain in encounters with non-animal physical objects (trees, rocks, etc.), in being afflicted with disease (from some organism, deficiency of diet, etc.), in encounters with other animals, and in encounters with man. We assume that every instance of each one of these types of encounters occurs because God has provided man with the *ideal* environment for becoming and living as a son (of God) and as a brother (to his fellow-man).

Since it was necessary (as I have explained already) for man to have a *physical* body, and since it was further necessary that that body be subject to *injury* and *death* (this world is not man's ultimate home), it was also necessary that man be placed in an environment which supplied the *needs* of that particular sort of body. Man has need for: air, water, food, clothing, shelter, aid in healing when injured or diseased, etc. Even though it may be possible for men to live without meat and skins, animals are a vital element in the totality of what God has supplied for man in his total environment, the *ideal* "vale of soul-making."

Man needs *food* to eat. Animals constitute a valuable source of food. Man needs *clothing*. The skins and wool of animals has supplied man with such from the beginning of man until the present time. In some cases man can feed and clothe himself without causing the animal to experience pain or injuring it in any way. But such is not always the case. Man kills and eats: antelope, cattle, fish, etc. And, man has long used the skins of animals to clothe and shelter himself. Of course, this requires the *death* of the animal.

VI. WHAT SHOULD WE CONCLUDE FROM THESE FACTS?

God is not something less than perfectly good because he created man with the *need* for *food*. God would not have been a better God if he had created man so that he would not need any food at all. We should draw such conclusions, because it is better for man, during his *probationary* period that he face the *challenge* of having to *plan, work* and *struggle* in order to supply his family and himself with food and other physical necessities. It would *not* be a *better* world than it now is if man had absolutely no physical needs to meet. In our present world, man is faced with the *challenge* of providing for the physical needs of his family and himself. An environment which involves such a challenge is better than one which does not. It is the kind of environment man needs for the development of fortitude, steadfastness, virtue, etc. Even more will be said later on human suffering of the value of this factor in man's total environment.

Animals have also been of great value to man (especially so, prior to modern technological developments) in providing *power* (for the accomplishment of work) and *transportation* (of both man and his possessions).

I have already noted that the ability to experience pain is of value to the animal *itself*. I now wish to note that the ability of animals to experience pain is of great value to *man*. One of man's greatest physical needs is to accumulate knowledge of the ills of his own body: what *causes* them, what will *cure* them. The fact that animals share a great commonality, in various physical attributes (including that of being able to experience *pain*) with man, means that animals can be a great instrument in the advancement of *medical science*. It is certain that man has presently advanced in medical science far beyond the point he would have reached if he had had no animals with which to experiment. Is it *evil* that God has provided man with such an instrument? Is it evil that man has used animals as such an instrument? Is it evil that *man* causes animals pain in his researches? Surely, it would be absurd to so contend. To be *consistent,* a critic would have to answer, "Yes," to these questions. (It might well be asked: "If God had provided man with no such instrument, would the critic of Biblical theism have used this lack as ground for claiming that God does not exist?") But I submit to you that the atheist would be wrong in answering, "Yes," to these questions.

In the light of plain Bible teaching, it is clear that there is a higher purpose to man than is fulfilled in this life[48] and that it was in harmony with the infinite knowledge, power, and goodness of God for him to provide man with such an instrument, and that it is right for man to use animals as such an instrument.

Thus far, two questions have been considered: Would it be a better world if there were *no* animals at all, and if there must be animals, would it be better if these animals could not *experience* pain? I have shown how we may answer both these questions negatively.

[48]Mark 10: 29, 30; 1 John 2: 15-17.

But the question might be raised: Is it *evil* for one animal to kill and eat another animal? Given the Biblical definition of evil (sin—the violation of God's will), I hold that it is *not* evil for, say, a lion to kill and eat an antelope. That such things occur is neither intrinsically good nor intrinsically evil, but reflects simply the state of nature, a state which we have found to be necessary for the "vale of soul-making." It is not evil *per se* either for a lion to kill and eat an antelope or for a man to kill and eat a pig. Such things occur simply as elements in the totality of the environment which God has provided for man in which to make his decision either to love God (and thus to enjoy fellowship with him as a son of God) or to reject God (and thus to fail to have that fellowship); that is, they are *instrumental* to providing man with as good a "vale of soul-making" as could be provided by an infinite knowledge, goodness, and power.

It seems clear that the atheist should refrain from objecting to one animal killing another animal until he himself stops killing animals. This would mean that no atheist, so long as he claims that one animal killing another animal in order to have food is evil, can continue to eat the meat of animals without branding *himself* as evil! It seems that any atheist who raises the objection which I have just been considering would live entirely on vegetables (plant life). But even here a question might be raised as to whether the destruction of plant life is evil. And, if the atheist can eat neither animal flesh nor plant life, what then could he eat? This throws him back on claiming that to even have a physical body is an evil situation. But upon what *grounds* could he make such a claim?

Before leaving this matter, I should like to point out—in far too brief a way—that the existence of animals in this world affords God a medium of teaching various spiritual truths to man. This is done both by statements in the Bible and by man's careful observation of and thought about animals. The Bible contains many references to animals of various kinds which make it clear that God expects man to learn profound moral and spiritual lessons from animals.

It should be remembered that my effort has not been that of presenting philosophic proof of these matters relating to animal pain. Rather, using the procedure of "faith seeking understanding," in the light of plain Bible teaching, I have shown that the proposition I have affirmed relative to animal pain can be affirmed along with the proposition affirming the infinite goodness and power of God without affirming a logical contradiction. J. L. Mackie has claimed (by implication, at least) that such could *not* be done, but it is clear to me that I *have* done it.

I have not claimed to have proved philosophically that animal pain is not evil; I have shown that, according to Bible teaching, it is not evil and have shown how this view fits into the total theodicy as I have set it out. I have shown that animal pain plays a vital role (serves a useful function) in the world as a "vale of soul-making." Beyond these matters, I have no responsibility in refuting Mackie's claim to have proved that the God of Biblical theism does not exist. To do what I have done is to provide a refutation of Mackie's claim.

It thus seems plausible to regard proposition W9 ("Every instance of animal pain results from some condition(s) which was necessary for providing man with the ideal 'vale of soul-making' ") as true. Since this is the case, the critic has no right to deduce (from the fact that animal pain occurs) the conclusion that no infinite God exists.

Chapter VIII

My Basic Affirmation and Human Suffering

In this chapter, I shall be concerned with: setting out the propositions which are relevant to this topic, explaining the relation of proposition W9 to these propositions, setting out the causes of suffering, explaining how human suffering relates to the characteristics of the ideal environment for "soul-making," considering objections which might be raised thereto, and explicating the conclusions which I draw from this discussion.

I. THE PROPOSITIONS WHICH ARE RELEVANT TO THIS TOPIC

Proposition W10 says, "Every instance of human suffering results from some condition(s) which was necessary to providing man with the ideal environment for 'soul-making.'" Proposition W10a says, "God is not blameworthy for having created a world in which innocent, righteous, and wicked persons suffer during their life in it." Proposition W10b says, "God is not blameworthy for having created a world in which there seems to be dysteleological suffering." My task in connection with the explication of these three propositions is to explain them in such fashion as to avoid any logical contradiction with the basic propositions of Biblical theism.

II. THE RELATION OF PROPOSITION W9 TO THESE PROPOSITIONS

In the explication of proposition W9, I have already set

out the basic characteristics of the ideal environment for "soul-making." It must be one which: supplies man's basic *needs,* allows man to be a *free* moral agent, allows man to be truly *challenged,* and allows man to *learn* what he most needs to learn about his earthly life. In connection with the explication of propositions W9, W12, and W11, I have discussed in some depth all of these three basic characteristics and how they relate: in general terms, to an ideal world; to natural calamities; and to animal pain. These characteristics must now be discussed, with some necessary repetition, in connection with the problem of human suffering.

III. THE CAUSES OF SUFFERING

It will be helpful first to list at least some of the *causes* of human suffering. Some suffering results from the carelessness or indifference of oneself or of some other person. Men are free to be careless and thoughtless. At times, such freedom results in intense and prolonged suffering. Some suffering results from ignorance. Other suffering results from one's own evil (sin). Men contract disease because of fornication, spend years in prison because of robbery, etc. Still other suffering results from the sins of others, e.g., a loving wife and her children are beaten unmercifully by a drunken husband. Men suffer and die from disease, earthquakes, tornadoes, etc. Men are devoured by wild animals. And in the light of Bible teaching, we learn that God in at least the sense that he has provided an environment in which such occurs, sends chastening upon men in an effort to lead them to become true sons of God and brothers of men.[49]

It is clear that much of man's suffering results from the free will of man—freedom to act: carelessly, ignorantly, lustfully, irrationally, maliciously, etc.

---

[49]Hebrews 12: 5-11; Psalm 94: 12; James 1: 12; Revelation 3: 19.

IV. HOW HUMAN SUFFERING RELATES TO THE CHARACTERISTICS OF THE IDEAL ENVIRONMENT

I have already discussed thoroughly that the *ideal environment* is one which allows man to be a free moral agent. In explication of proposition W9, W12, and W11, I have shown that this means that man's *environment must* be a law-abiding one (man must be able to depend upon his environment to respond with regularity) and that this means that "mutual interferences" (destruction) *can* occur with land, with property, with plants, with animals, and with men.

Further, I have argued that for man's environment to allow him to be a free moral agent, it must be one which allows the proper "epistemic distance" between man and God. In that connection, I have explained that God provided man with a physical body and placed him to live among other physical entities in a physical environment (the world). I have argued that the proper "epistemic distance" means that man must not be so *close* (epistemically—i.e., "distance" related to *knowledge*) to God that he is so *overwhelmed* by the immediate presence of Deity (or by the *evidence* for him) that it is *impossible* for him to *avoid* believing in God, and that he must not be so *far away* (epistemically) from God that he cannot be *drawn to* God by the evidence provided for him in that environment.

I have shown further how natural calamities and animal pain are related to fulfilling man's basic needs, allowing him to be truly free, allowing him to be challenged, and allowing him to learn certain basic things which he needs to learn. It remains now to show how human suffering is related to these characteristics of the ideal environment.

There is no need for anything to be said further on the matter of our evironment being able to fulfill man's physical needs.

Much has already been said in regard to the matter of the ideal environment allowing men to be free moral agents. I have discussed at some length the view that man's environment must be a law-abiding one. However, it would be worthwhile to recall that since man has a *physical* body living in a *physical* environment in which there are other physical entities, there *must* be the possibility of "mutual interferences" (occasions on which some sort of *destruction* occurs). Thus, man of necessity is subject to injury and, as a result, is subject to suffering. Much of man's suffering comes as a result of his own ignorance and/or carelessness. Much suffering results from poor emotional life, which leads to organic disease. Men are free to react to problems with fear and worry rather than with fortitude and courage. Such freedom makes possible suffering which is both *intense* and *prolonged*.

Many men suffer because of *other* men—men who will not *become* and *live* as true sons of God and brothers of men. Individual men mistreat other individuals: they rob them, they steal their property, they slander their good names, they seduce their daughters and wives, they incarcerate them unjustly, etc. Nations have mistreated other nations. Races of men have mistreated other races of men. Those of certain political views have persecuted those of differing political views.

It seems incredible that the leaders of one ethnic group would do to another ethnic group what the German Nazis did to the Jews at such extermination camps as Belsen and Auschwitz during World War II. Many have asked, "Why did not God prevent this?"

If man is to be truly free, it *must* be *possible* for such things to happen. I have argued previously that not even *Omnipotence* can prevent a man from mistreating his neighbor without infringing upon his character as a free moral agent. As surely as there are free moral agents living in a law-abiding physical world (so that when a lead bullet is shot at a man's head destruction will follow) there *must* be the *possibility* of human suffering (as well as animal pain).

If bricks are to have the physical characteristics which enable men to build houses out of them, and if the world is to be law-abiding (which it must be to be the environment for rational and moral action), then it must be *possible* also for one man (a free moral agent) to use a brick to crush the skull of another man.

It must be *possible* for suffering to be *intense* and *prolonged*. This is the case because, if men are to be free, they must be free to be evil. And, given this freedom, some men degenerate to be as evil as were the Nazis, who so hated the Jews that they wished to degrade, insult, de-humanize, and even exterminate them. Since this is the case, the existence of even the most intense and prolonged suffering cannot be grounds for concluding that God does not exist.

The ideal environment for man must be one which allows him to be *challenged*. Man was placed in an environment which offered him the great challenge to learn its secrets, to "gain dominion" over it. Knowledge of the world in which he lives was not given miraculously to man nor was it set out in books for him to learn. He had to gain that knowledge and record it in books for himself. Man faced the challenge of learning about and building better means of transportation than walking or riding an animal. He has responded to that challenge by building machines with sufficient power, by gaining sufficient overall knowledge, and by developing the skills required to span not only the greatest oceans in a matter of hours but to fly to the moon and back to earth again. It is not the technological advances *per se* which are truly crucial at this point but the *challenge* to make these advances. Because of such accomplishments, men around the world were inspired and filled with determination to make their own lives more meaningful. But they would *not* have been so inspired if the necessary knowledge and skills had simply been *given* to man *without* any effort at all upon his part. If the men who made the flight to the moon had not faced the necessity of gaining knowledge and developing skills, and if, making that flight had involved absolutely no danger (of severe injury, suffering or death) to them, other men would not have been so thrilled and inspired by their feat. If man's environment did not provide situations in which he faced the possibility of suffering some truly terrible loss (of property, well-being, life), then it would not provide a situation in which such virtues as fortitude and courage could be developed as they now are. These facts make it clear that the *ideal* environment for man is one which makes it possible for man to suffer—and, not merely to suffer, but to suffer *intensely*. And, it must not only allow men to suffer intensely, but to suffer intensely over a *long period* of time. This particular point is closely related to the possibility of developing sympathy, which I shall discuss later in this chapter.

The ideal environment is one which allows man to face the challenge of becoming a true son of God. The basic purpose of human life is to have the opportunity of becoming a true (spiritual) son of God. There is a sense (since God is the creator of men) in which every man is a son of God. But reference is here made to those who, seeing and understanding the evidence for God and understanding his will, are willing to submit completely to him in obedience to his will. God is Creator, the Ruler (Sovereign) and, in the light of Bible teaching, it is clear that he will be Judge (through his Son, Jesus Christ) of all men.[50] But this is not all: he wishes to be the *Father* of all men. If he is Father to a man, then that man will be his *son*. This means that the son will submit completely to the Father no matter what the cost may be.[51] One must submit completely to his will (which is found in the Scriptures) when one's situation is

[50]Hebrews 9: 27; Acts 17: 30, 31; Romans 2: 16.
[51]Revelation 2: 10; Hebrews 11: 24-26; Luke 14: 26-33.

72

one of health, prosperity, happiness, etc. Further one must submit to his will even when he is suffering. When one concludes that his suffering is due to chastening (from the Father) then he must submit meekly (as should a child to the necessary discipline administered by his loving fleshly father), examining his motives and actions to see wherein corrections need to be made in order to conform to the Father's will.

When one concludes that he is suffering (being persecuted by evil men) for being a loving son of the Father, then he should rejoice that he has such a privilege and that his sincerity and devotion have been noted by the enemies of the father.[52]

When suffering comes in the midst of such circumstances that he cannot decide whether he is being *chastened* (for acting in a way which is unbecoming to a son of God) or being persecuted (because he *is* a living, obedient son of God), then he must *trust* God, as his Father, to have designed his environment so that he has some morally sufficient reason (providing him a "vale of soul-making" for having created a situation in which such events could occur. One must say, in effect, "Even though I die, yet will I trust him.[53] No matter what may be the situation in which one suffers, one should, as a son, perceive the benefits of living in an environment in which such suffering can occur.[54] There is no compelling reason why the son of God should not believe this.

The ideal environment is one in which one can face the great challenge of becoming and living as a true *brother* to his follow-man. There is a sense in which one is a (spiritual) brother *only* to those who have become (spiritual) sons of God.[55] But there is also the sense in which one is the

---

[52]Matthew 5: 10-13.
[53]Job 13: 15; Proverbs 3: 5, 6.
[54]Romans 8: 28.
[55]John 1: 11-13; Galatians 3: 26, 27; John 3: 3-5.

(fleshly) brother to every other man (since God is the crea-tor of man).[56] It is this latter sense to which special refer-ence is here made. Every son of God should strive to be a true neighbor (one who helps in time of need) to his fel-low-man.[57]

The Bible teaches that Jesus Christ, the Son of God, is our perfect example.[58] He accepted and submitted to the will of God without reservation—even to the point of giving his life on the cross. Nor was this submission for his own welfare (he had no sins) but for the good of others.[59] Jesus was the Son of God, but he was also a "brother" to men. To be true sons of God, men must *strive* to *imitate* the perfect example of Christ.[60]

Following the example of Christ, sons of God are to "empty" themselves (rid themselves of self-centeredness) and be willing to live their lives for the benefit of others.[61] Becoming *absorbed* in living as a son of God always includes —never excludes—being a "brother" (neighbor) to one's fel-low-man.

To be a true son of God and a true brother to men, one must react to instances of suffering so as to demonstrate his trust in and love for God to those who are not yet sons of God. The ideal environment for "soul-making" must be one in which this kind of "tug" toward God can occur in view of those who are not sons of God; that is, those who are not yet sons of God must live in an environment which affords them the opportunity of observing how true sons of God react in trusting *submission* (to God), to their *own* suffering, and in loving *service* to *others* who suffer. This involves the fur-ther case of the non-son of God being the one who suffers. What is the son of God to do when one who is not a spiritual

[56]Genesis 1, 2.
[57]Luke 10: 25-37; Romans 12: 20, 21.
[58]Hebrews 4: 15; 1 Peter 2: 20, 21.
[59]Hebrews 2: 9.
[60]Matthew 5: 43-48.
[61]Philippians 2: 5-8.

74

son of God suffers? It likely will do little good for the son of God to tell the non-son, "I am trusting in God that there is a morally sufficient reason for *your* suffering." It would be valuable, of course, for *some* explanation to be attempted, but, even beyond that, it would be vital for the son of God to do what he can to *help* the non-son (who is suffering) in any way he can—and to give this help in *love* and *compassion*. "When our difficulties evoke our personal trust, and when others' difficulties evoke our loving service, the very difficulties that *seem* to deny God's Fatherhood bring it out more fully. How do they? Because *trust* is the proof of our sonship, and *service* is the proof of our brotherhood."[62] No environment which eliminated completely the *possibility* that men could suffer—even *intensely* and over a *long period* of time—could be the ideal environment in which man is to make his decision either for or against God.

Further, the ideal environment must offer man the challenge to suffer and endure malicious persecution without maliciously striking back.[63] Again, given the perfect example of Jesus Christ as the model of proper reaction to suffering,[64] men should not react to ill-treatment by hating or mistreating those who persecute them. Such response affords a basis for profound spiritual and moral refinement and growth. But to respond to ill-treatment in the spirit of revenge (maliciously desiring the hurt of one's persecutor) is to involve oneself in a course of attitude and action which is destructive of moral and spiritual progress. The suffering of oneself and of one's fellow-man affords one an opportunity either for growth in love and compassion for others or for doing that which is destructive of love and compassion and, thus, of moral and spiritual progress. Surely, no environment could be the ideal "vale of soul-making" if it did not offer this possibility.

[62]Edwin Lewis, *op. cit.*, p. 23.
[63]Romans 12: 20, 21.
[64]1 Peter 2: 21-23.

75

The ideal environment for "soul-making" must be one which allows man to *learn* the things he needs most to learn about life on earth.

First, he needs to learn that life on earth is both *certain* and *uncertain*. It has an element of *certainty* (in that it is certain that it will come to an end—man will die). Man's sojourn on earth is limited; the earth is *not* his *ultimate* or final home. The citizenship of the true son of God is in *heaven*. Man's life on earth has an element of *uncertainty* in that it is uncertain as to *when* it will end. No one knows exactly the day or the hour when he will die. Thus, not knowing when he will die, he does not know when his period of probation will end. This ignorance should stimulate each man to strive to be in right standing with God every moment of his earthly life.

Second, man needs to learn that life on earth is both *significant* and *insignificant*. It is *significant* in that it is the *one* and *only* probationary period during which man makes his decision as to whether to become a son of God. No decision can be made relative to this matter *after* this earthly life is over. Man's earthly life is *insignificant* in regard to the trials, adversities, and sufferings which he endures during it. The consequences of man's decision either to become a son of God or not to become a son are of such magnitude as to render all of these sufferings of no ultimate negative significance. It will no doubt be the case that when men reach heaven, they will be amazed to recall that they ever grumbled or doubted while in the midst of suffering while on earth. They will say that even if their suffering had been a million times worse than it was, it still would have been no more than "the snap of a finger" in comparison with the grandeur and glory now experienced (full, ultimate fellowship with God).[65]

Further we learn (from plain Bible teaching) that the

---

[65]2 Corinthians 4: 17, 18; Revelation 21, 22.

punishments of hell will be of such magnitude that one will say that even if the sufferings of earthly life were a million times worse than they actually were, they still would not be significant in comparison with what one suffers in hell (final, ultimate loss of fellowship with God).[66]

The Scriptures make clear that existence in either heaven or hell will be un-ending.[67]   Thus the conditions in each situation will be both of great magnitude (beyond present human comprehension) and unending.

V. OBJECTIONS WHICH MIGHT BE RAISED

Before drawing final conclusions relative to human suffering, it would be well to consider some objections which might be raised against the views set out above: objections as to *distribution* of suffering, objections as to *amount* of suffering, and objections as to *failures* of suffering to result in "soul-making"—that in spite of the suffering in the world, some people fail to become sons of God.

1. *Objections as to distribution.*   Under this heading, there are at least three basic objections: no one can explain the teleological connection of each and every instance of suffering; even though infants cannot profit morally or spiritually from such, yet they suffer; and often righteous men suffer more intensely and longer than do wicked men.

It would be ridiculous to hold that any mere man could ever attain to such knowledge as would enable him to explain in specific detail all of the teleological connections of *every* instance of human suffering. But, from the teachings of the Scriptures, we can see that God has given us, through Jesus, a *model* for suffering. It is clear that God has a morally sufficient reason for having created the world in which human suffering *can* occur: viz., that *every* instance of human suffering results from some condition(s) which was necessary to providing man with the ideal environment for

---

[66]Revelation 20: 10-15; Mark 9: 47, 48; 2 Thessalonians 1: 7-9.
[67]Matthew 25: 46.

"soul-making" (Proposition W10). Thus, we can have confidence: that God does *not* let us suffer because of (his) *meanness* (lack of love), that he does *not* let us suffer because of (his) *ignorance* (lack of knowledge), and that he does *not* let us suffer because of (his) *weakness* (lack of power). He lacks neither love, nor knowledge, nor power. There is nothing in the nature of the world in which we live to *forbid* our believing this. The Bible plainly teaches that we should believe it.

It is, of course, true that infants (who are perfectly innocent of *any* wrong-doing) suffer, at times, and even die. Based upon this fact, the objection is raised that this world is not the ideal "vale of soul-making" (with the *implication* that the world would be *better* for such purposes if *only* wicked persons suffered, and if each person suffered only in the intensity and duration which his wrong-doing *deserved*).

In reply, I note that the objection is based upon: a *misconception* of what is the case with all suffering, and either *ignorance* of or *rejection* of his Son. It is simply not the case that all suffering is punishment for sin.[68] The righteous and innocent sometimes suffer. This is the case because there is need for "randomness" as an element in the totality of the "vale of soul-making" that is, there must be an element of unpredictability as to which persons will experience adversity. If it were the case that one could *avoid* any and all adversity (pain, disease, suffering, etc.) by simply becoming a (spiritual) son of God,[69] then man would not be living in an ideal environment for soul-making for the simple reason that he would not have a situation in which a *challenge* would be involved in his decision to become a son of God. Men would be tempted to become sons of God solely in order to escape having cancer, being injured or killed in an automobile accident, etc. Becoming a

---

[68]John 9: 1-3; Luke 13: 1-5.

[69]That is, being "born again": John 3: 1-5; Galatians 3: 26, 27; Romans 6: 3-5.

son of God must involve the challenge of possible suffering because of such decision. If it were the case that becoming a son of God eliminated all possibility of suffering, then this world would not be the ideal environment for "soul-making."

It is also true that, in some instances, *righteous* men suffer *longer* and *more intensely* than do very *wicked* men. Based upon this fact, the objection is raised that this world cannot then be an ideal environment for "soul-making." In reply, I note that the same basic arguments used in reply to the objection related to the suffering of infants also applies in this instance: there must be an element of "randomness" (non-predictability as to who will suffer and how much) in the matter of human suffering. In the case of the suffering of righteous persons (spiritual sons of God) there is the added factor that the sufferer himself can profit from the suffering. Suffering can be a value even to the faithful son of God: there are some "mountains" of spiritual attainment which can be reached best by going down through the "valleys" which lie in front of them. The son of God thus can see better that this life will soon be over, that the truly important things in human life pertain to the soul (of himself and of his neighbor), etc. and thus be helped to a better understanding and appreciation of the love of God.

In the case of the son of God who has drifted into unfaithfulness (i.e., conduct unbecoming to a son of God and a brother of man has become characteristic of him), there is an element of *chastening* involved in his suffering. If God "speaks softly" to man by evidence of himself in the natural world, he *cries out* to man (by providing him with an environment in which it is possible for such things to occur) to recognize, love, and submit to him when pain and suffering occur. Suffering, then, in such cases is an instrument designed to lead man to realize that he has made a tragic mistake in forsaking his place as a son of God and to return to living as a son and a brother.

2. *Objections as to amount*. Objections as to *amount* are of two sorts: Why is there *any* at all? And why is there *so much* (such intense and prolonged) suffering? In my estimation, my discussion of other specific problems really constitutes a reply to this objection. I have shown that our environment would be something less than ideal if it were not at least *possible* for *very intense* and *very prolonged* suffering to occur in it. Since man is a free moral agent, he is free to act carelessly, ignorantly, irrationally, lustfully, maliciously, etc. And, since this is the case, he is free to be the cause of both very *intense* and very *prolonged* suffering. The Nazis could not have been truly free moral agents if they had not been free to set up and operate such places as Auschwitz and Belsen.

The part played by natural calamities and animal action in the total picture I have explicated already.

3. *Objection relating to failure*. The objection relating to *failure* also can take the form of a question: if human suffering is related vitally to "soul-making," why are there so many *failures?* Why do so many people *reject* God in spite of the claimed moral and spiritual value of pain and suffering? In reply, I refer once again to the fact that man is a free moral agent. As such, not even Omnipotence can *guarantee* a favorable reaction to the various influences he uses to persuade man toward becoming and living as a son of God and brother to man. Suffering is an "instrument" which man may *use* (respond to in a *proper* way) or *mis-use* (respond to in an *improper* way). An illustration of this point may be helpful: a very sharp knife is an instrument which man may *use* (to his own *profit)* or mis-use (to his own *hurt;* the crucial factor is whether he grasps the knife by the *handle* or the *blade.* The fact that man is free makes it possible for him to decide to grasp the knife by the blade instead of by the handle. If it were *impossible* for him to decide to take the knife by the blade, then he would *not* be

free. So it is with suffering: if man were *not* free to decide to react to pain and suffering with *resentment* and *rebellion* (rather than with *humility* and *loving submission* to God and greater *compassion* and *service* for his brother), then he would not be a truly *free* moral agent. By making the implied claim that man should have been guarded absolutely against a wrong reaction to suffering, one really is pleading that man should not be a free moral agent. And in pleading that man should not be a free moral agent, one is actually pleading that *man* should no exist at all!

Surely, no total environment which did not allow man the freedom to react improperly to suffering can be viewed rightly as the ideal one for "soul-making."

VI. CONCLUSIONS ON HUMAN SUFFERING

By way of summation of and conclusion from the material which I have discussed on human suffering, I now consider: the benefits (value of) suffering, proper reaction to suffering, summation as to the essential matters which have been shown.

Some of the *benefits* of suffering are: it allows a life of self-denial, which is the greatest life; it allows opportunity for God to "cry out" to men in the effort to lead them to become true (spiritual) sons of God (the hearts of men are either the most tender or the most bitter during times of severe tribulation); it affords opportunity for one to develop and grow in moral character (fortitude, virtue, courage, etc.); it affords opportunity for man's love for God and man to be *tested* in the finest possible way (one must choose *suffering* over *sin);* it affords exceptional influence in bringing the wayward back to God (suffering tends to be highly conducive to leading such men to re-evaluate their attitudes and actions); it affords the basic ground for growth in compassion and love for one's fellowman; it helps one to better appreciate the love which he has for others and which others have for him; it helps man to better understand and appreciate the love of God for him and his own love for God; and it will help him to better appreciate the grandeur of heaven in the life to come.

For the non-son of God, the proper *reaction* to suffering is to be brought to God by it, in humility and loving trust. For the son of God the proper reaction to suffering is: in cases of *chastening* (when wayward) one should submit meekly to the chastening and return, in sincere penitence, to God; in cases of *persecution* (for righteousness' sake), one should rejoice that he is allowed so to suffer; in all cases in which one *cannot be certain* whether the suffering is chastening (for a wayward son) or persecution (for being such a faithful son) one should simply trust that this world is as good as any possible world and, thus, that God has a morally sufficient reason for what is occurring; when the son himself is suffering, he should strive to bear *his own* burden; when others are suffering, one should seek eagerly to help them bear *their* burden; in all cases, one should cast his burden on God (trust in God for an adequate solution); and in all cases, one should strive to *learn* from suffering what God would have him to learn.[70]

It is in order to state some final *conclusions* in regard to suffering. It seems clear that there is *no* compelling reason why we should not but *many* compelling ones as to why we should believe: that it is in harmony with the infinity of God that man should have a probationary life in a world in which it is possible for him to experience pain and suffering, that pain and suffering are things for which we in this life should thank God, that pain and suffering are things without which (during earthly life) the lives of men would be worse than they are, that pain and suffering are things which mark our ultimate relationship with the crucified Son of God, that pain and suffering *per se* are not really evil, that only that which is unfilial and unfraternal is really evil,

---

[70]Romans 8: 28.

82

and that no logical contradiction is involved in the conjunction of these propositions with the remainder of the basic propositions of Christian theism.

Chapter IX

My Basic Affirmation and Man's Final Destiny

Three propositions will be discussed in this chapter: W13, W14, and W15. These propositions are quite crucial to my basic affirmation.

I. PROPOSITION W13

Proposition W13 says, "Man's earthly life is a probationary period during which his fate in eternity is settled." In the light of plain Bible teaching, we hold that this present world was designed by God to be the environment in which man (a free moral agent) makes his decision either to accept fellowship with God (by virtue of faithful, loving obedience to his will) or to reject that fellowship. The basic purpose of human life on this earth is to make that decision. Man will have no occasion of making such a decision after his life on earth is over. This proposition will be basic to this entire matter of man's eternal destiny.

II. PROPOSITION W14

Proposition W14 says, "Man is immortal; that is, he will live on after physical death in a non-probationary period which is non-ending." To hold that one can be saved (become a son of God, and thus entering into fellowship with God), in some life *after* physical death, from the consequences of the evil he has committed during earthly life, is to deny the *significance* of man's life in this present world. And, if man's life in this present world is not significant (that is, if it is not *crucial* to deciding his eternal destiny) then it seems that pain and suffering during this life *cannot* be justified. If man's eternal destiny can be decided *without* the probationary period of *earthly life,* but in some later probationary period, then the pain and suffering which man experiences during earthly life appears pointless and meaningless. And, if God planned such a pointless and meaningless existence for man, then he is surely deficient in at least one (and perhaps all) of these attributes: power, knowledge, and goodness. From plain Bible teaching, we learn that man's life on earth is a probationary period during which his fate in eternity is settled and that man will live on after physical death in a non-probationary period which is nonending.[71]

III. PROPOSITION W15

Proposition W15 says, "The 'stakes' in eternity (the blessings of heaven and the punishments of hell) are of such magnitude as to render all pain and suffering in this life of no ultimate negative significance." Christian faith holds that the tribulations of this present are not worthy to be compared with the blessing of eternal fellowship with God in heaven.[72] Even if one were to gain all of the money, land, houses, etc. which the world offers, all of the praises which men can offer, absolute power over every individual in every nation on earth, the opportunity to indulge himself in every possible form of sensual pleasure, etc. such gain would be insignificant in comparison with either the gaining of eternal fellowship with God in heaven, or the eternal loss, in hell, of fellowship with God.[73] These "blessings" weigh as nothing in comparison with the blessing of ultimate fellowship with God. The length of earthly life is but

---

[71]Hebrews 9: 27; Matthew 25: 30-46; Revelation 20: 10-15; Luke 16: 19-21.

[72]Romans 8: 18; 2 Corinthians 4: 17; Hebrews 11: 24-26, 35; 1 Peter 1: 6, 7.

[73]Matthew 16: 26; Luke 14: 26-33; Mark 10: 28-31.

a moment in comparison with the eternity in which one shall either enjoy the fellowship of God or else suffer the loss of that fellowship eternally.[74]

[74]2 Corinthians 4: 17; Matthew 25: 46.

Chapter X

My Basic Affirmation and Some Crucial Questions As To What Is Good and What Is Evil

At this point, consideration will be given to what has already been said on the matter of what is good and what is evil. Also, some of this material will be elucidated further. In this connection, first, some questions as to what is good and what is evil will be raised and answered. Second, some matters which illustrate the answers will be set out. Third, some more questions will be considered. Fourth, a number of conclusions regarding good and evil will be stated. And, fifth, a word will be said about how all of this relates to this thesis.

I. SOME QUESTIONS AS TO WHAT IS GOOD AND WHAT IS EVIL

One pertinent question is: What is *intrinsically good* (that is, what is good in and of itself, and an *end* and *not* merely as a *means* to an end)?[75] Vital to the proper answer to this question is the recognition of God's purpose in creating man; viz., for *sonship* (with *himself*) and, concomitantly, for *brotherhood* (with his *fellow-man*). Thus, whatever is *filial* and *fraternal* is *intrinsically good*. It is intrinsically good to believe in God, to love God, to honor God, to obey God. It is intrinsically good to *become* a son of God and to *live* as a son of God. Whatever is filial and/or fraternal can never, under any circumstances, be evil.

---

[75]Consider: Matthew 19: 17.

A second question is: What is *intrinsically evil?* Only that is *intrinsically evil* which is *unfilial* and/or *unfraternal.* It is intrinsically evil to reject God, to fail to love God, to rebel against God, to refuse to honor and obey God, to be self-centered rather than God-centered. It is intrinsically evil to fail to be a son of God, to be out of fellowship with God. It can never be good, in any sort of circumstance, to be unfilial and/or unfraternal.

A third relevant question is: What is *instrumentally good?* That which helps to bring about or to bring to pass that which is filial and/or fraternal is instrumentally good. To say that something is instrumentally good is to say that it is good as a *means,* not that it is good as an *end* within and of itself.

A fourth question is: What is *instrumentally evil?* That which hinders that which is filial and/or fraternal is instrumentally evil.

A fifth question is: What is to be *valued?* Only that is properly valued which is either intrinsically good or instrumentally good. Nothing which is either intrinsically evil or instrumentally evil should ever, under any circumstances, be valued.

II. SOME MATTERS WHICH ILLUSTRATE MY ANSWERS

A critic might contend that the answers given above will not do as a *practical* solution to the problem. He might ask such a question as this: How would you fit into your scheme such matters as money, houses, lands, good health, pleasure, recreation, murder, rape, peace of mind, pain during surgery, pain during illness, pain encountered accidentally, love and marriage, becoming a parent, being persecuted for righteousness' sake, tornadoes, hurricanes, earthquakes, a lion killing and eating an antelope, heaven, and hell? Are these matters intrinsically good or intrinsically evil? Are they instrumentally good or instrumentally evil? Are they to be valued or disvalued?

For the purposes of this series of lectures, I can say that there are only about seven or eight *classes* of things listed above: material possession, states of mind (attitudes), natural calamities (tornadoes, etc.), animal pain, human suffering, recreational activities, family activities, family relationships, and human sin. Since most of these matters in principle have already been discussed in detail, it would not only be repetitive but useless to go over the same ground again. However, it seems there would be some value in considering some *specific* instances of some of these matters and how these might be explained in harmony with my basic thesis. In connection with each one of these specifics, it should be recalled that a thought, action, etc. is to be regarded as *intrinsically* good if and only if, it is filial and/or fraternal. It is to be regarded as *instrumentally* good if it helps to bring about or to continue that which is filial and/or fraternal. Whatever helps recognition of fatherhood (of God), sonship, and brotherhood is instrumentally good.

So, if some critic asks, "What about good health, is it good or evil? Is it to be valued or disvalued?" the answer must be given in terms of whether or not the matter about which he inquires is filial and/or fraternal or it helps that which is filial and/or fraternal. Good health is not intrinsically good, for it *can* be the means of *hindering* sonship and brotherhood. It is possible for a man to become so enamored of his good health, of the strength and power of his body, that his good health actually becomes a barrier to his becoming a son of God. On the other hand, if one's possession of good health contributes to an attitude of thanksgiving (thus leading him in the direction of sonship and brotherhood), then that good health is instrumentally good. In such a case, it is to be valued. Good health is *not* to be valued when it becomes a *barrier* to sonship and brotherhood.

Let it be further supposed that a critic asks, "What about pain during surgery? Is it not the case that such is intrinsically evil? Is it not the case that every person wishes to avoid it (and thus asks for an anesthetic)? And, if pain during surgery is intrinsically evil, is it not the case that your contention (that nothing sub-human is intrinsically evil) is false?" It should be recalled that all of the section which explicates the proposition that the world was created by God to be the ideal environment for soul-making is relevant to the question raised here. We live in a world which was designed to be the kind of world in which it is possible for pain and suffering to occur. (The value of the world being this kind of world has been explained already.) If it were not possible for pain to occur (for instance, in the case of an appendix which is about to burst), then one would not even know of the *need* for surgery. And, if one is to have pain as a warning of the need for surgery, then it must be the case that surgery (without anesthesia) will involve pain. The value (in developing feelings of sympathy) of pain and suffering in fellow-human beings has been explained already. More important questions to be raised are: Is the pain of surgery itself evil? Is the surgeon who inflicts the pain evil? Certainly the surgeon is not evil for inflicting pain while saving a man's life. The pain itself is neither filial nor unfilial. Thus, the pain itself is neither intrinsically good nor intrinsically evil. However, if the pain is instrumental in helping him who experiences the pain to advance in the direction of sonship and brotherhood (as it often does), then it is instrumentally good. If it hinders such an advance (e.g., in causing the person to reject the view that God is perfect in goodness), then it is instrumentally evil. In cases when pain is instrumentally good, it is to be valued. In cases when it is instrumentally evil, it is to be disvalued. Nothing which hinders sonship and/or brotherhood is to be valued.

If the critic raises the question as to whether *sensual pleasure* is good *per se,* the answer must be basically the same as that given to the questions set out above. Sensual pleasure *per se* is neither intrinsically good nor intrinsically evil. Let sexual intercourse, as a classic instance of sensual pleasure be considered. Sexual intercourse *per se* between a man and a woman is neither intrinsically good nor intrinsically evil. If such intercourse is either *premarital* or *extramarital,* then it is, in the light of Bible teaching, in violation of God's will and is, thus, intrinsically evil.[76] And, it is possible for sexual intercourse even within marriage to be instrumentally evil. If, say, Mr. and Mrs. X place such a great emphasis upon such physical pleasure that they are caused to forget God, then such intercourse is instrumentally evil. Or, if Mr. X, allows himself to become so enamored of sexual activity that he comes to regard his wife as merely an *instrument* (for his own satisfaction) rather than as a *person,* then, for him, sexual intercourse has become instrumentally evil. This is the case because, for him, such activity has led to that which is unfraternal and, thus, infilial.[77]

As a final instance, let it be supposed that the critic raises this question: "What about the case of a Christian being thrown to (and devoured by) the lions only because he will not make a statement to the effect that he does *not* believe that Jesus of Nazareth is the Son of God? Surely you must admit that it is intrinsically evil for one to die so horrible a death only because he will not make a certain statement." The total situation involving a Christian being thrown to the lions is a complex one, involving a number of constituent elements: the hungry lions, the Christian, the persons who made the decision that he should be devoured by the beasts, the persons who threw him to the beasts, the act of throwing (or forcing) him to the beasts, etc. The lions are not evil; they act in harmony with the nature which God has

---

[76]Galatians 5: 19-21; Ephesians 5: 3, 4.
[77]1 Corinthians 13: 1-7; 7: 1-5; Ephesians 5: 23-33; 1 Peter 3: 7.

given them. They are not capable of sonship and/or brotherhood. Thus, their act of devouring the Christian was neither an intrinsic evil nor an instrumental one. It was not evil for the Christian to refuse to renounce his faith; rather, being filial (an act of loving obedience to God) it was intrinsically good. However, the decision to throw him to the lions, being both unfilial and unfraternal (disobedience to the will of God) was intrinsically evil. The pain and suffering (on the part of the Christian) was an instrumental good in that it brought the Christian even closer to God (enhanced his filial relationship). Thus it is seen to be possible that that which is *good* (obedience to God) can be the source of *pain* and that that which is *evil* (disobeying God) can be the source of *pleasure* (the experience of the persecutors in throwing the Christian to the lions).

So goes the basic argument in regard to all of the matters which were listed in the objections set out above.

III. SOME MORE QUESTIONS CONSIDERED

In connection with the foregoing paragraphs, a number of other questions might be asked: Is my basic affirmation (explicated) a *justification* of the claim that physical evil does not exist? Do the special solutions to the problem of animal pain count as a defense of that claim? How much of the problem of evil is solved by denying that there is physical evil?

My basic affirmation, as I have set it out in this discussion, is *not* a *justification* (in the sense of *philosophic proof*) of the claim that there is no such thing as "physical evil." As I noted earlier in this discussion, the procedure used in setting out my basic affirmation is that of "faith seeking understanding"; that is, given Biblical faith, we raise the question: Can the concepts of the basic propositions of Biblical theism be so interpreted and so explicated as to avoid both affirming a logical contradiction (in the conjunction of the propositions of Christian theism) and having to accept a weakened version of theism (for instance, having to accept the view that God is either limited in power or limited in goodness)? J. L. Mackie has charged that such interpretation and explication of these propositions *cannot* be accomplished. He admits, however, that *if* it could be done, his claim to have disproved (by the use of the problem of evil) the existence of the infinite God will have been overthrown. So, a basic point in this discussion has been that, given Biblical faith, the claim that intrinsic evil on the purely physical level does not exist is a vital part of that faith, and the conjunction of the propositions involving that claim and the rest of the propositions of Christian faith do *not* involve a logical contradiction. So, even though my basic affirmation (as I have set it out in these lectures) does not constitute a justification (in the sense of philosophic proof) of the claim that physical evil does not exist (in the intrinsic sense), it *does* constitute a *kind of justification* of that claim in that it meets Mackie's challenge and overthrows it.

The positions I have taken in this discussion relative to *animal pain* are based on the same procedure: "faith seeking understanding." Given Biblical faith, the propositions relative to animal pain can be fitted into the total picture (the conjunction of all of the relevant propositions of Christian faith) *without* a logical contradiction. In this sense, the special solutions to the problem of animal pain set out in this discussion count as a defense of the claim that intrinsic physical evil does not exist.

As to the question of *how much* of the problem of evil is solved by the claim that intrinsic physical evil does not exist, it must be made clear that I have made no claim that the problem of evil is solved by any given *isolated* proposition (relative to some specific problem such as animal pain) but by my basic affirmation (which I explicated earlier) itself, which encompasses twenty-two specific propositions. It is the interpretation and explication of the concepts of these propositions in such fashion as to avoid their conjunction involving a logical contradiction which solves the problem, at least insofar as the refutation of Mackie's challenge is concerned. And, the refutation of Mackie's challenge is the basic problem with which I have been concerned all along. The claim that evil does not exist on the purely physical level is a vital element in the totality of the twenty-two propositions involved in this thesis. The thesis would not stand without this element. But, on the other hand, the claim that intrinsic evil does not exist on the purely physical level would not solve the problem alone; "solving" the problem requires the totality of all twenty-two propositions involved in the thesis.

IV. SOME CONCLUSIONS REGARDING
GOOD AND EVIL

From the matters previously discussed, I draw a number of conclusions. First, vital to this problem is the Biblical view that God created man for sonship and brotherhood, for recognition of his fatherhood, for fellowship with him. Second, whatever is filial and fraternal (whatever is lovingly obedient to God), whatever truly involves recognition of the fatherhood of God, whatever truly involves fellowship with God is *intrinsically good*. Whatever human action is in harmony with the will of God is intrinsically good and can *never,* under *any* circumstance, be either intrinsically or instrumentally evil. Third, whatever is unfilial and unfraternal (whatever is truly disobedient to God), whatever truly rejects recognition of the fatherhood of God, whatever truly involves rejection of fellowship with God is *intrinsically evil*. Whatever human action is in violation of the will of God is intrinsically evil and can *never,* under *any* circumstance, be either intrinsically or instrumentally good. Fourth, whatever *helps* sonship and brotherhood is *instrumentally good*. Fifth, whatever *hinders* sonship, and brotherhood is *instrumentally evil*. Sixth, no mere object, no mere event, no living thing which is sub-human can be intrinsically evil.   Seventh, heaven is intrinsically good because it is the ultimate of sonship and fellowship with God.[78]   Eighth, hell is intrinsically evil because it is the ultimate in the loss of sonship and fellowship with God.[79] And, ninth, whatever is either intrinsically or instrumentally good should be *valued,* and whatever is either intrinsically or instrumentally evil should be *disvalued.*

V. HOW THIS CHAPTER RELATES TO MY BASIC AFFIRMATION

In the light of the foregoing material in this section, the question might be asked, "What, exactly have you accomplished by your contention that only that is intrinsically evil which is unfilial and/or fraternal?"   In taking this position, I accomplish the following.

First, because this view is basic to all of the other facets of my thesis, it helps me to counter the basic contention of the atheist.   That basic contention is that God (whose existence is counter-factual to his belief) is evil (at best, not infinite in goodness) because he made a world in which occur evil things (for which he alone is responsible).   But my thesis rejects this conclusion by rejecting the premises from which it is drawn.   It is true that there is evil in the world, but it is not evil for which *God* is blameworthy.   Everything which God created was good, including man.   Man, by the misuse of his own free will, was guilty of sin (disobedience, that which is unfilial).   Man, not God, is blameworthy for man's sin.   By showing that such matters as natural calamities, animal pain, and human suffering are not intrinsically evil, I protect the view that God is not blameworthy for anything.   In doing so, I show that the problem of evil cannot be used to prove that the infinite God does not exist.

Second, this position prevents my having to "give ground" on the view that God is infinite in *both* power and

---

[78]Revelation 21, 22.
[79]Revelation 20: 10-15; 2 Thessalonians 1: 79; Matthew 25: 46.

goodness. The position thus prevents my having to accept a weakened version of theism. Since, given Christian faith, God created the world to be the ideal "vale of soul-making" for man, and since God made the world in such fashion that natural calamities, animal pain, and human suffering (some instances of which have nothing whatever to do with a misuse of man's free will) occur in it, if these matters are intrinsically evil, then God is evil for having created such a world. In showing that these matters are not intrinsically evil, I am enabled to *reject* the conclusion that God is *not* perfect in goodness.

Third, it enables me to argue the case in harmony with the purpose of God in creating man and the world. God created man for sonship (with himself) and, concomitantly, for brotherhood (with his fellow-man). It is God's will that every person be a son and a brother and, thus, that every thought and every deed of every person be filial and/or fraternal. Human life is for sonship and brotherhood; plant life and animal life (as well as the world) are for man. Thus, man's life on earth constitutes his opportunity to become and live as a son of God. This means that earthly life is the opportunity for man to submit to God without reservation, accepting and obeying his will no matter what might be involved. And, proper submission to God involves an attitude of fraternity toward one's neighbor. Fatherhood, sonship, and brotherhood all must be kept in proper perspective. Only the God-centered man (who, of course loves his neighbor) is saved. The selfish, self-centered man is lost (out of fellowship with God). Only the filial, fraternal man is saved (in fellowship with God). The unfilial, unfraternal man is lost (not in fellowship with God).

Chapter XI

Conclusion

I. WHAT HAS BEEN ACCOMPLISHED?

In the preceding seven sections the positive element of my thesis has been explicated, showing that the conjunction of the propositions of Christian theism which are pertinent to the problem of evil does not involve a logical contradiction. Thus, this explication constitutes a refutation of Mackie's claim to have proved that no infinite God exists.

During the course of explicating the twenty-two propositions involved in the seven topics of the *positive* element, I also have established the *negative* element of my thesis. I have done this by showing that at least some of the propositions crucial to Mackie's case have been shown to be false (or, at the best, very doubtful) and that, hence, he has not established the conclusion which he deduces from these propositions.

Thus, I have clearly established the truthfulness of my basic thesis, for I have established both the positive and negative elements of that basic thesis.[80]

I hold that my basic affirmation (thesis) (with its *positive* and *negative* elements) is adequate as a refutation to this atheistic challenge for at least three reasons. First, my

---

[80]Even though it does not strictly belong to this particular series of lectures, there is still another element of my basic thesis; viz., the counter element. The counter element is stated as follows: the affirmation of the basic propositions of atheism (as regards the so-called "problem of evil") involves a logical contradiction: therefore, atheism cannot be true. But the discussion of this element must await another book which, the Lord willing, I plan to write.

thesis affirms all of the basic attributes of God (perfect in power, knowledge, goodness, justice, etc.) without giving ground on any of them. Second, my thesis affirms that *sin* is the *only* evil (and thus avoids the view that God himself uses *evil means*—natural calamities, animal pain, and human suffering—to attain *good ends*) and, thus, that God is not blameworthy in any sense. And, third, it emphasizes the insignificance of the *amount* and the distribution of suffering without giving ground on the significance of the world as a "vale of soul-making" and of man's earthly life as his one and only probationary period, and thus shows that no one can point to lengthy and intense suffering and properly conclude: "There is no God."

II. MY FINAL CLAIMS

Further, by the use of the *positive* element of that thesis, I have shown that the conjunction of the basic propositions of Christian theism does *not* involve a logical contradiction, as Mackie claimed it did. And, finally, by the use of the *negative* element of my own thesis, I have shown that Mackie has *not* established his claim to have shown that traditional theism involves a logical contradiction.[81]

Since this is the case, then Mackie's challenge has been dissolved. It thus turns out that he has not used the existence of evil in this present world to prove that God does not exist. This is the basic conclusion from the foregoing discussion. In a positive way, proof of the existence of God *can* be set out, but that remains for another work which, the Lord willing, I plan to attempt.

In a future work which I plan to do, I hope to show that it is the affirmation of *atheism*—not that of Biblical theism—which involves a logical contradiction.

Selected Bibliography

Books

Augustine, Aurelius. "On Free Will," in John H. Burleigh Editor, *Augustine: Early Writings*. Philadelphia: The Westminster Press, 1953. Vol. VI, Library of Christian Classics, pp. 102-217.

Bakan, David. *Disease, Pain and Sacrifice*. Chicago: University of Chicago Press, 1968.

Bales, James D. *The Biblical Doctrine of God*. West Monroe, Louisiana: Central Printers and Publishers, 1966.

Bledsoe, A. T. *A Theodicy*: or *Vindication of the Divine Glory*. New York: Carlton and Porter, 1853.

Brightman, Edgar Sheffield. *A Philosophy of Religion*. New York: Prentice-Hall, Inc., 1940.

Buber, Martin. *Good and Evil*. New York: Charles Scribner's Sons, 1952.

Burton, Marion L. *The Problem of Evil*. Chicago: The Court Publishing Company, 1909.

Buttrick, George Arthur. *God, Pain and Evil*. Nashville, Tennessee: Abingdon Press, 1966.

Camus, Albert. *The Plague*. New York: Random House, 1948.

Casserley, J. V. L. *Man's Pain and God's Goodness*. New York: Morehouse-Goreham Company, 1951.

Davidson, A. B., ed. *The Book of Job*. Cambridge: University Press, 1886.

Dommeyer, Frederick C., ed. *Current Philosophical Issues*. Springfield, Illinois: 1966.

Ducasse, C. J. *A Philosophical Scrutiny of Religion.* New York: The Ronald Press Company, 1953.

Fairbairn, A. M. *The Philosophy of the Christian Religion.* London: Macmillan, 1902. pp. 513.

Farrer, Austin. *Love Almighty and Ills Unlimited.* Garden City, New York: Doubleday and Company, Inc., 1961.

Ferré, Nels F. S. *Evil and the Christian Faith.* New York: Harper and Brothers, Publishers, 1947.

Flew, Antony, and MacIntyre, Alasdair, eds. *New Essays in Philosophical Theology.* New York: Macmillan Company, 1955.

Flint, Robert. *Anti-Theistic Theories.* 6th Edition. Edinburgh: William Blackwood and Sons, 1899.

Forsyth, P. T. *The Justification of God.* London: Duckworth and Co., 1916.

Hartshorne, Charles, and Reese, William L. *Philosophers Speak of God.* Chicago: University of Chicago Press, 1953.

Hartshorne, Charles. *The Divine Relativity.* New Haven, Connecticut: Yale University Press, 1948.

Hick, John. *Evil and the God of Love.* New York: Harper and Row, Publishers. 1966.

Hinton, James. *The Mystery of Pain.* New York: D. Appleton and Co., 1892.

Joad, C. E. M. *God and Evil.* London: Faber and Faber Limited, 1942.

Journet, Charles. *The Meaning of Evil.* Translated by Michael Barry. New York: P. J. Kenedy and Sons, 1963.

Jung, C. G. *Answer to Job.* Cleveland and New York: The World Publishing Company, 1967.

King, Albion Roy. *The Problem of Evil.* New York: Ronald Press, 1952.

Leibniz, Gottfried W. *Theodicy: Essays on the Goodness of God, the Freedom of Man, and the Origin of Evil.* Translated by E. M. Huggard. New Haven: Yale University Press, 1952.

Lepp, Ignace. *Atheism in Our Time.* Translated by Bernard Murchland. New York: Macmillan Company, 1963.

Lewis, C. S.. *The Problem of Pain.* New York: Macmillan Company, 1948.

Lovejoy, Arthur O. *The Great Chain of Being.* New York: Harper and Row, Publishers, 1936.

MacIntyre, Alasdair C. *Difficulties in Christian Belief.* New York: Philosophical Library, 1959.

McTaggart, John E. *Some Dogmas of Religion.* Chapter 6 and 7. London: Edward Arnold, Ltd., 1906.

Madden, Edward H., and Hare, Peter H. *Evil and the Concept of God.* Springfield, Illinois: Charles C. Thomas, Publisher, 1968.

Maritian, Jacques. *God and the Permission of Evil.* Translated by Joseph W. Evans. Milwaukee: Bruce Publishing Company, 1966.

——————. *St. Thomas and the Problem of Evil.* Milwaukee: Marquette University Press, 1942.

Marty, Martin E. *Varieties of Unbelief.* Garden City, New York: Doubleday and Company, Inc., 1964.

Mascall, E. L. *He Who Is.* London: Longmans, Green and Co., 1943.

Matson, Wallace I. *The Existence of God.* Ithaca, New York: Cornell University Press, 1965.

Milligan, R. *An Exposition and Defense of the Scheme of Redemption.* 11th edition. St. Louis: Christian Board of Publication, n.d.

Munk, Arthur W. *Perplexing Problems of Religion.* St. Louis, Missouri: Bethany Press, 1954.

Murray, John Courtney. *The Problem of God.* New Haven: Yale University Press, 1964.

Orr, James. *The Christian View of God and the World.* Grand Rapids, Michigan: Wm. B. Eerdmans Publishing Company, 1960.

Petit, Francois. *The Problem of Evil.* Translated from the French by Christopher Williams. New York: Hawthorn Books, Publishers, 1959.

Pike, Nelson, ed. *God and Evil.* Englewood Cliffs, New Jersey: Prentice-Hall, Inc., 1964.

Rashdall, Hastings. *The Theory of Good and Evil.* Vol. II. London: Oxford University Press, 1924.

Robinson, H. Wheeler. *Suffering Human and Divine.* New York: The Macmillan Co., 1939.

Royce, Josiah. *Religious Aspects of Philosophy.* Chapter 22. New York: Harper and Row, Publishers, 1885.

——————. *Studies of Good and Evil.* Hamden, Connecticut: Archon Books, 1964.

Russell, Bertrand. *Why I Am Not a Christian.* New York: Simon and Schuster, 1957.

Siwek, Paul. *The Philosophy of Evil.* New York: The Ronald Press, 1951.

Sontag, Frederick. *Divine Perfection.* New York: Harper and Brothers, Publishers, 1962.

Stanley, Jones E. *Victory Through Surrender.* New York: Abingdon Press, 1966.

Taylor, A. E. *The Problem of Evil.* London: Ernest Been, 1929.

Tsanoff, R. A. *The Nature of Evil.* New York: The Macmillan Co., 1931.

Voltaire. *Candide.* Edited by Haskell M. Block. New York: The Modern Library, 1956.

Weatherhead, Leslie D. *Why Do Men Suffer?* New York: Abingdon Press, 1963.

—————. *The Will of God.* New York: Abingdon-Cokesbury Press, 1954.

Webb, Bruno, O. S. B. *Why Does God Permit Evil?* London: Bloomsbury Publications, 1959.

Whale, J. S. *The Christian Answer to the Problem of Evil.* New York: Abingdon Press, 1936.

Articles from Books

Campbell, A. "Address on Demonology," *Popular Lectures and Addresses.* Nashville, Tennessee: Harbinger Book Club, 1861.

Kaufmann, Walter. "Suffering and the Bible," *Faith of a Heretic.* Garden City, New York: Doubleday and Company, Inc., 1961.

McTaggart, John. "God, Evil, and Immortality," *Religion from Tolstoy to Camus,* ed. by Walter Kaufmann. New York: Harper and Row, Publishers, 1964.

Plantinga, Alvin. "The Problem of Evil," in *God and Other Minds.* Ithaca: Cornell University Press, 1968.

Articles in Dictionaries and Encyclopedias

Abelson, J. "Righteousness (Jewish)." *Encyclopedia of Religion and Ethics.* 1908-1922. Vol. X.

Bertocci, Peter A. "Attributes of God." *Encyclopedia of Religion.* 1964.

Brightman, S. S. "Evil." *Encyclopedia of Religion.* 1964. 1 vol.

Clark, Gordon H. "God." *Dictionary of Theology,* 1960.

—————. "The Divine Attributes." *Dictionary of Theology.* 1960.

Dungan, David Roberts. "Evil." *International Standard Bible Encyclopedia.* 1947. Vol. II.

Evans, William. "Wrath." *The International Standard Bible Encyclopedia.* 1947. Vol. V.

Goddard, B. L. "Justice." *Dictionary of Theology.* 1960.

Morris, Leon. "Eternal Punishment." *Dictionary of Theology.* 1960.

MacAlister, Alex. "Pain." *The International Standard Bible Encyclopedia.* 1947. Vol. IV.

McConnell, Francis J. "Righteousness." *The International Standard Bible Encyclopedia.* 1947. Vol. IV.

MacKenzie, J. S. "Infinity." *Encyclopedia of Religion and Ethics.* 1908-1922. Vol. VII.

Orr, James. "Punishment Everlasting." *The International Standard Bible Encyclopedia.* 1947.

Owen, H. P. "Infinity in Theology and Metaphysics." *The Encyclopedia of Philosophy.* 1967. Vol. IV.

Packer, James I. "Just, Justify, Justification." *Dictionary of Theology.* 1960.

Rees, T. "God." *The International Standard Bible Encyclopaedia.* 1947. Vol. II.

Robinson, W. C. "Wrath." *Dictionary of Theology.* 1960.

Taylor, A. E. "Theism." *Encyclopedia of Religion and Ethics.* 1908-1922. Vol. XII.

Articles from Journals

Aiken, Henry David. "God and Evil." *Ethics,* LXVIII (January, 1958), 77-97.

Farrell, P. M. "Evil and Omnipotence." *Mind,* LXVII (July, 1958), 399-403.

Frankfurt, H. G. "The Logic of Omnipotence." *The Philosophical Review,* LXXIII (1964), 262-72.

Graves, S. A. "On Evil and Omnipotence. *Mind*, LXV, No. 258 (April, 1956), 259-62.

Keene, G. B. "A Simpler Solution to the Paradox of Omnipotence." *Mind*, LXIX, No. 273 (January, 1960), 74-75.

Mackie, J. L. "Evil and Omnipotence." *Mind*, LXVII (July, 1958), 399-403.

McCloskey, H. J. "God and Evil." *Philosophical Quarterly*, IV, No. 39 (April, 1960), 97-114.

Pike, Nelson. "God and Evil: A Reconsideration." *Ethics*, LXVIII, No. 2 (January, 1958), 116-24.

Ramsey, I. T. "The Paradox of Omnipotence." *Mind*, LXV (April, 1956), 263-66.

Smart, Ninian. "Omnipotence, Evil and Supermen." *Philosophy*, XXXVI, No. 137 (April and July, 1961), 188-95.